CRICKET
MY WAY

IAN BOTHAM

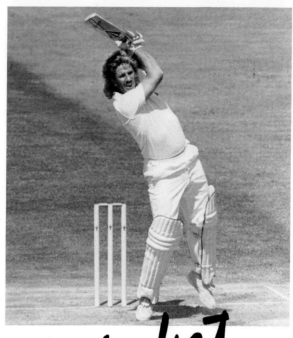

Cricket My Way

WITH JACK BANNISTER

WILLOW BOOKS
Collins
8 Grafton Street, London W1
1989

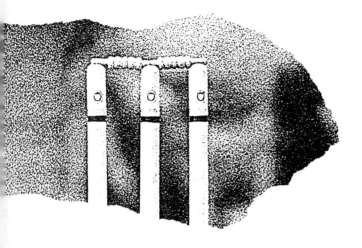

Willow Books
William Collins Sons & Co. Ltd
London · Glasgow · Sydney
Auckland · Toronto · Johannesburg

First published 1989
© Newschoice Ltd and Ian Botham 1989
Photographs courtesy of Adrian Murrell/All-Sport and Patrick Eagar
Design by Graham Davis Associates
Illustrations by John Scorey

British Library Cataloguing in Publication Data
Botham, Ian, *1955–*
    Cricket my way.
    1. Cricket
    I. Title   II. Bannister, Jack
    796.35′8
    ISBN 0-00-218315-3 (Paperback)
    ISBN 0-00-218348-X (Hardback)

Typeset by Ace Filmsetting Ltd, Frome, Somerset
Printed and bound in Great Britain by
Mackays of Chatham, Letchworth

CONTENTS

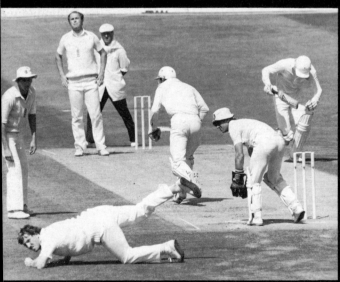

PREFACE

The Headingley electronic scoreboard of 18 July 1981 flashed that historic bookmaking quotation of 500–1 against England beating Australia—and that is why I am writing this book. Not just to re-hash that famous England win, but to try to explain to all cricketers why they should *never ever accept the result of any match as a foregone conclusion.*

Cricket is just not like that, and although that Test match provided a once-in-a-lifetime fairy story ending, I have played in plenty of other matches where a game has suddenly been tilted unexpectedly because one player had the guts to attack against all the odds.

My approach to cricket is simple. Give me a challenge and I'll take it on. If there's no challenge, then I try to find one. I know my strengths—and weaknesses—and I have always set goals for myself from school right through to Test cricket. And when I've achieved something I set out to do, I immediately re-set the goalposts. That is the best way I know to sustain enthusiasm, and no matter at what level you play the game, there is so much more fun to be got out of cricket, if you give yourself something really demanding to aim at.

Never mind if you fail. Part of the point of sport is that there are winners and losers. What you have to do is to convince yourself that you are going to be a winner more often than not, and you'll be surprised at what sometimes happens. In this book I shall try to explain the correct technical approach to every part of the game—batting, bowling, fielding, wicket-keeping, captaincy—but my main message will be much more fundamental.

The real basis of any cricketer's success has got to be attitude, and I want to show how properly used aggression can help any player in the world.

From my early schooldays at Milford Junior School and Bucklers Mead School, I decided I wanted to be the best, and so I had to think, talk and play like the best. I am naturally aggressive—in fact, my whole way of life is based on aggression, mostly I hope of the right sort.

Like lots of kids, I wanted to bat and bowl so that I was always in the game, but most allrounders soon decide that is too much like hard work and so become batsmen who bowl, or the other way around. But by sticking at it, I gave myself the extra opportunity to be centre stage throughout a match with two strings to my bow.

The first actual coaching I remember was from a teacher, Ken Hibbert, when I was about eight or nine. It was all to do with the grip, and after all—just like golf—if you get the grip right you've got chances. Get it wrong, and just forget it, because it will lead to a repetition of basic errors which will prevent any consistent success.

Like every part of cricket, *the best is the simplest.* The bat was laid down in front of me, and I was told to pick it up as though I was going to chop a piece of wood. Instinctively my hands came together. That

'Give me a challenge and I'll take it on.' In this instance against the Australians—perhaps my favourite opponents.

11

is, quite simply, the most important tip of all to any young batsman. It doesn't really matter whether the hands are at the top or the bottom of the handle, as long as they are together.

I soon found I could hit the ball hard and often, and even when I came into contact with my first county cricketers, nobody tried to alter my basics—simply because they were correct.

When I was about 11, Dad captained the Westlands 2nd XI—after playing a lot for the first team—and I used to travel with him. When certain guys used to go to the Taunton nets, I went with them, and I well remember Kenny Palmer there. He used to spend a lot of time encouraging me in a net by dragging me off on my own and throwing a few balls to me. I think he had a soft spot for me, and in fact he still does.

Remember the scene at Headingley against Pakistan in 1987 after their wicket-keeper Salim Youssuf claimed that 'catch'. Kenny was at point and came in like the speed of light to defuse what could have been quite an incident. I like to think he did that because he knows I have always tried to play the game in the right way—but more of that later.

So it was Dad, Ken Hibbert and Ken Palmer early on, and then Harry Sharpe, Tom Cartwright and Brian Close later, who were the main influences on my career. I still ring Tom up, because he taught me all the basics in bowling, when not many people saw anything in me in that department. For instance, when I went on to the Lord's Ground Staff in 1972 at the age of 16, their attitude was that I was only a batsman. Harry Sharpe thought I might be a bowler, but Len Muncer didn't.

They had a lot of specialist bowlers so I was naturally regarded as a batsman who could bowl to members. My reaction was 'I'll show 'em.' So when I went back to Somerset and Tom offered to show me a few things, I listened—another example of working out for yourself who and what is right for you. That is something nobody can teach you, but I shall try to explain certain of the basics which should never alter. As an example, Tom taught me how to swing the ball both ways, although I had always found the outswinger came quite naturally to me.

That is my first tip. Decide on what you want, and then go for it. Don't be put off by failure or criticism.

I soon found out that, done properly, cricket is a simple game. I was lucky enough to start with because I found it natural to hold the bat and the ball correctly, and no matter what anyone else says, the real secret of my success is that I play the game in a much more orthodox way than most people realize. For instance, I hit mainly straight, with great emphasis on my leading left arm and hand. With the ball I have worked hard on my hand and wrist action, which is why I hit the seam so often and can also swing the ball. In the slips, I may look inattentive sometimes, and not everyone agrees with the way I stand with hands on knees, *but I stand still, and concentrate on each ball as hard as I can.*

Once you know the basics, the rest is down to *attitude*. Create a belief in yourself, and stay true to it—even through the bad spells that come to everyone.

Cricket is a great leveller, but don't let it push you into a routine mould where you suddenly forget to aim for the top.

To sum up my own attitude, which I always try to carry into my batting and bowling, my philosophy is 'Where can I score runs off the next ball?' whereas too many batsmen—even county players—seem to think 'How can I avoid being out to the next ball?' And with bowling my first thought is 'How can I take a wicket with this ball?' compared with the reverse approach of 'How can I best bowl a maiden?'

Many people see me as a spontaneous cricketer. I am not completely that, because that would make me just as much a blinkered cricketer as someone whose approach is too cautious. I never am blinkered; I am always trying to work out how best to attack the opposition.

There is a huge difference between correct and incorrect techniques. There is just as big a difference between sensible, controlled aggression and the other sort.

This book is to explain those differences.

PART

ONE

HOW I PLAY MY CRICKET

Happy days at Somerset during my 60-ball century v Worcester, at Weston-super-Mare, 1986.

Hooking Imran Khan, Fourth Test, England v Pakistan, Edgbaston, July 1987. If you are going to hit the ball, hit it hard.

People are always asking me if I ever had any coaching or instruction. Of course I did, but where I was lucky was that nobody ever tried to meddle with whatever came naturally to me.

The main message of this book is to listen to all the advice offered to you, because it is well meaning, and then decide what will work for you.

The first two real influences on me were my Dad, Les, and then a sports master called Ken Hibbert at Milford Junior School. Dad used to throw a few balls to me when I was only three or four, and as long as I played straight, he never attempted to force anything else on me.

One example of how vital the proper advice can be came to me at the tender age of nine. I was playing against Westfield—another junior school in Yeovil—and I nailed a left-hander right in front of the stumps with a big inswinger to him. Because I didn't know what leg before wicket, l.b.w., meant, I didn't appeal. At the end of the over Ken Hibbert, who was umpiring, asked me: 'Why didn't you appeal?' I said, 'For what? He didn't hit it and I didn't bowl him.' Of course I had heard about 'l.b.w.'

but I simply didn't have a clue what it meant.

Ken only explained to me once, and from then on I got a packet of them—mostly with my away swinger which was my natural ball.

Looking back on my progress on to the Somerset staff in 1973, I now realize that I was lucky enough to strike the right balance between going my own way, and absorbing the right sort of advice and coaching which was aimed at maximizing my natural talents, but *not* at the expense of stifling my natural aggressive approach with bat and ball.

I have always tried to hit the ball hard, and I have always tried to take wickets. Now let me try to pass on the tips which have helped me most.

All of them won't suit every young cricketer, just as every piece of advice given me was not taken, but I guarantee that if I can get over my attacking philosophy, *any cricketer can only benefit from what I have learned*. For instance, I have tried to be such a complete allrounder that I could justify selection with either bat or ball.

Trevor Bailey has gone on record as saying, 'Botham is our most spectacular, dynamic and suc-

cessful allrounder in Test cricket this century. His only serious rival is the immortal W. G. Grace from the previous one.'

What a double billing that makes—'Grace & Botham'—or should I insist on alphabetical order!

I have often been criticized for attacking too much with the ball, but the plain truth is that I have always been prepared to gamble a few runs away for a wicket, whereas some bowlers simply do not have that attacking streak in their make-up. For instance, Mike Hendrick was a fine bowler, with all the attributes of line and length, stemming from a lovely high, sideways action. Yet in 23 Tests for England he never took five wickets in an innings.

My bowling is always aimed at taking wickets, and I am always prepared to try a slower ball, or a bouncer. As well, of course, as using the width of the return crease to increase the batsman's problems with a different angle of delivery.

There are so many variations for a seam bowler to try, and he should never settle for containment, even on a flat pitch. That is, unless the state of the game calls for a 'mean spell'.

With the bat, when I attack—which is most of the time—I reckon the safest way is to play and hit straight. My margin of error is greater because every time a batsman plays with a crooked bat, he is reducing his area of contact with the ball.

Again Trevor Bailey was kind enough to comment: 'In my career, I encountered very few hitters, and nobody in the same class as Ian Botham. His straight back stroke, whether used for defence or offence, is mainly with the full face, while his feet are in the correct position and his downswing from the top of the full backswing is copybook.'

I also remember Alan Smith, the England manager of the 1981 tour of the West Indies which I captained, telling me that I could play as straight as anyone in the game, and that was my real strength.

Before I move on to the detail of technique, let me summarize my attitude, which I have had through every level of cricket I have played: I only want to win, and am prepared to gamble when others are not. Sometimes it comes off and my side wins a match from nowhere, and then I'm a hero in the public's eye. But sometimes, my side loses a match we might have drawn, and then I get plenty of stick. I only want to win and hate losing. Coming second is nothing; *but you have to lose sometime, and then comes the next test of character.*

Some dressing rooms become morgues, and I cannot understand that—not if everyone has done his best. I try to use defeat as a spur for the next game. My motto is to have a drink with the enemy and get on with life. I always wanted to be a winner. That is why my approach is based on an unshakable confidence in my own ability never to back off, and always to attack when there is the slightest chance of affecting the course of a match.

Even as a kid, I would not compromise my approach, and because I have never accepted the idea of defeat, we pulled through.

It sounds so obvious to say 'never give up', but so often the temptation is overwhelming to accept the cards dealt you. *Resist it always, and you will be amazed at how much more you will enjoy the game.*

BOTHAM ON THE ATTACK

'A fair example of that is one of my first games in 1974 in the Benson and Hedges quarter-final on June 12th at Taunton against Hampshire.

'What a glorious twelfth it turned out to be, even though it cost me a few broken teeth from an *Andy Roberts bouncer. Needing 183, we were 113 for 8, with Roberts still to bowl seven overs.*

'The game was gone—nearly. I notched a 45 not out, we won the game, and the lesson is there for all to see.'

PART

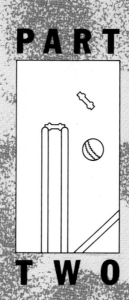

TWO

BATTING

1
HOLDING THE BAT

THE GRIP The most important part of batting is for a batsman to find out for himself the most comfortable way of holding the bat and standing at the crease. *Grip, stance and back-lift are the key to everything, and if they are not mastered, the rest of batting becomes more and more difficult.*

There are one or two golden rules, but not half as many as the average coaches say. If they were right then everyone would hold the bat and stand at the crease in exactly the same way.

But they don't—just think for instance of the different stances of Peter Willey and Graham Gooch. Or Viv Richards and me, Mike Gatting and Allan Lamb, and so on. They have all worked out what suits them best, but although there are huge differences, certain basic details are common, and it is these I want to explain.

The orthodox grip should always have both hands together on the handle. Any photographs of me batting, whether hitting the ball hard and high or, much more rarely, playing defensively, invariably show how close together both hands are.

Ideally they should not be either at the very top or bottom of the handle, but if that makes you feel more comfortable, then don't be put off by a coach telling you to move them up or down.

If they stay together, there is a much better chance of them working together under the guiding control of the top hand, rather than letting the bottom hand take over.

Obviously the higher up the handle the hands are, the wider the arc that is created for the bat to swing through, and some batsmen move to the top later in an innings, when they are trying to accelerate.

Even if the hands are at the very bottom of the handle, although some power might be lost, there is a compensatory increase in control because the bat has effectively shortened. This is what golfers do when they sometimes 'choke down' on a particular club to tighten up control. Sticking with golf, the driver is the most difficult club in the bag to control, *because it is the longest club*; so always remember that the nearer the top the hands are, the greater will be the power factor—but at the expense of a little bit of control.

So don't hold it at the top, just because your particular hero does. I am pretty near the top—not quite all the way—simply because from the time I developed my first and only grip, that is what suited me best, and nobody tried to change me.

Once Ken Hibbert found out I naturally got hold of the bat in a reasonably correct way, he left me alone; so as soon as a batsman finds out by trial and error what suits him best, he must stay with it.

Of course, some good players do have their hands apart, but as with any successful orthodoxy, the batsman concerned succeeds in spite of, and not because of, any particular quirk.

Derek Randall comes to mind. He built a fine career with a grip based on his hands being further apart than any other top player I can remember. It helped his great strength of cutting, because that stroke is entirely governed and controlled by the bottom hand. But he could still drive with the best of them because he had the ability to relax the bottom hand and let the top hand take over when he attacked on the front foot.

Derek is a good example of how slavishly rigid coaching would have ruined a potential England player – what fun we would have missed!

Sport is choc-full of performers who apparently defy all the rules, and yet still deliver the goods. Lee Trevino in golf and Alex Higgins in snooker *appar-*

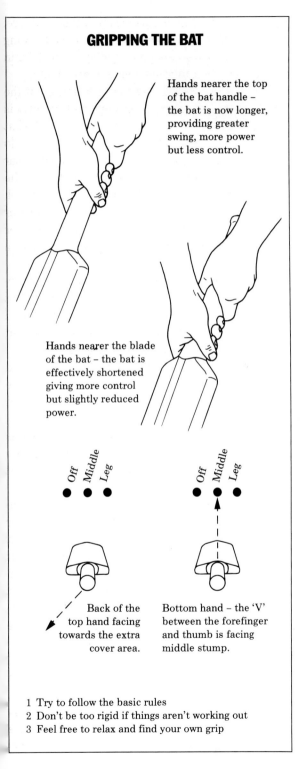

GRIPPING THE BAT

Hands nearer the top of the bat handle – the bat is now longer, providing greater swing, more power but less control.

Hands nearer the blade of the bat – the bat is effectively shortened giving more control but slightly reduced power.

Off   Middle   Leg

Off   Middle   Leg

Back of the top hand facing towards the extra cover area.

Bottom hand – the 'V' between the forefinger and thumb is facing middle stump.

1 Try to follow the basic rules
2 Don't be too rigid if things aren't working out
3 Feel free to relax and find your own grip

ently ignore the coaching manuals in much of what they do, but look at the results they have produced. Much of their set-up and preparation seems all wrong, but in spite of that, everything is right at the moment of impact through the ball; and cricket is no different. As long as the bat is accelerating straight through the line of the ball at impact, it really doesn't matter how you arrive there.

So to sum up the grip, do what I did. Lay a bat down on the ground, and just pick it up *with hands together* as though you are picking up an axe to chop wood. Remember that because the real power in wood-chopping as well as batting comes from both hands working together. The position of the top hand can vary a little, but as a general rule the back of the hand should face out towards extra cover.

A little variation either way won't hurt, but all sorts of problems arise if, for instance, the hand is turned round too much, with the back facing gully. As a check, *the 'V' between forefinger and thumb should face back on to middle stump*; whereas if the hand comes round further, it ends up facing fine leg, and it is almost impossible to drive off the front foot with that sort of set-up.

If the top hand—the left for the right-hander and vice versa for the 'caggies'—is turned round too much the other way, then the back of the hand faces the bowler, and it is impossible to get all the fingers round the handle.

Regarding the bottom hand, try and keep it as relaxed as possible, even if it means not wrapping all the fingers round the handle. I know a lot of players who just concentrate on holding the bat lightly, but firmly, with only the thumb and forefinger of the bottom hand on the grip. You need to be a real touch player to carry it that far. As a general rule, as long as the *'V' is in line with that of the top hand*, you won't go far wrong.

If all four fingers are on the handle, and it feels right, don't alter it, because the grip is the starting point of so much that is right or wrong in batting.

I have spent more time on the top hand than the other one because although I don't agree with much

A good illustration of top hand 'V' between forefinger and thumb, facing offside.

Derek Randall's unorthodox grip with the separated hands.

of the orthodox coaching teachings, I realize that cricket is mostly a sideways game, with the opposite hand and arm the governing influence. By that I mean, for the right-handed batsman, his top, leading left hand and arm is the most important one. Again there are plenty of top-class players with strong bottom grips—Allan Lamb comes to mind as one example. He has worked out what suits him best. Because he is shorter than me, he clearly cannot drive the same length deliveries as I can, and so that strong right hand has given him extra power for back foot strokes, like cutting and pulling.

A good illustration of the value of a correct grip. The leading left arm and top hand have totally controlled the stroke and kept the blade open to the offside. The right hand has supplied the power at impact and nothing else.

spoiled by the interference with their natural ability that over-coaching produces.

I've dealt with the grip, so now to the stance. Again I repeat, that what happens *before the ball is bowled*, settles much of what happens when the real action starts.

Let me explain the advantages to me of my own stance, which is quite 'spread'. By that I mean that my feet are further apart than the coaching manuals indicate is the ideal position. I stand that way because that is how I feel most comfortable, and that last word governs so much of my approach to batting, although it doesn't appear too often in the official teaching books.

THE STANCE When I spent my two years on the Lord's Ground Staff in 1972 and 1973, one of the coaches who never tried to alter my batting approach was Harry Sharpe. He would stand behind me in the nets, and would make the odd comment, but his general view was 'nine times out of ten you hit it where you want—so why change?'

Exactly, and if more coaches were as far-sighted as Harry, then fewer promising cricketers would be

Anybody who ever offered me any advice as a kid—including Dad, Ken Hibbert, Dave Burge and

THE STANCE

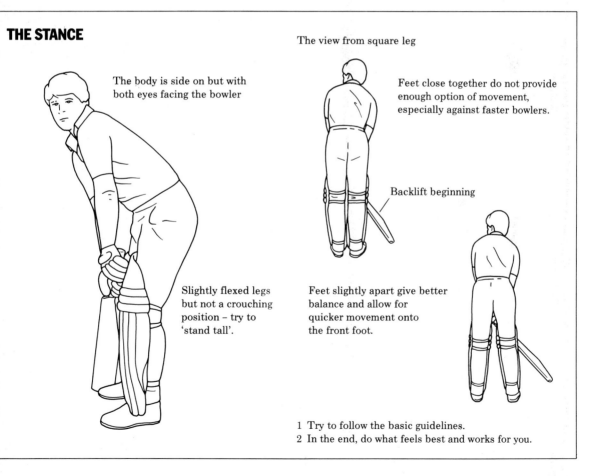

The view from square leg

The body is side on but with both eyes facing the bowler

Feet close together do not provide enough option of movement, especially against faster bowlers.

Backlift beginning

Slightly flexed legs but not a crouching position – try to 'stand tall'.

Feet slightly apart give better balance and allow for quicker movement onto the front foot.

1 Try to follow the basic guidelines.
2 In the end, do what feels best and works for you.

Graham Gooch, England
and Essex. An unusual
stance, but the raised bat
and straight legs work for
him. A perfect position of
head and level eyes.

Ivor Twiss— all used to accompany a particular tip with 'as long as you feel comfortable doing it'.

There is one technical advantage in a wider stance: *it cuts down unnecessary movement*. Most batting errors stem from incorrect movement of either feet or head, or both. For instance, if the feet are together against a really fast bowler the great majority of strokes will have to be off the back foot. So as well as valuable split seconds being lost in getting back on to the stumps, the whole body is on the move, and a ball coming at around 85 miles an hour over about 19 yards is difficult enough to keep out, even if you are in a correct position.

The position and alignment of the feet are aimed at producing a sideways stance, with the batting crease the ideal dividing line between the feet.

Standing 'spread', with the head still, cuts movement down to a minimum, as I soon worked out for myself—all because it felt comfortable. That magic word again.

In my opinion, the big disadvantage of standing with feet too close together is that the batsman has little balance. For instance, if you stand with both feet together it won't take a strong person to push you off balance with just a forefinger; but if you spread your feet you have a solid base to resist much more pressure.

The other thing to remember is not to stand too rigid. If you do, all sorts of movements have to take place before contact is attempted. To illustrate the point, there is another valid comparison to make in golf, which I think has a lot in common with batting, although one game involves a moving ball and the other does not. All the top pros go through the same routine in setting up for each shot, and they have a key which releases the backswing. Jack Nicklaus,

for instance, has that slight turn of the head to the right. There are players like Sam Torrance and Greg Norman who sometimes do not ground their club, because that makes their body too rigid.

The same with batting. Flex the knees slightly and make sure the body weight is evenly distributed, so that you can either play forward or back, dependent upon the length of the ball.

Try not to crouch; although there again there are plenty of successful batsmen in top cricket who don't 'stand tall' at the crease, and it works for them, crouching is not ideal.

A lot of nonsense is talked about a 'two-eyed' stance, which is supposed to mean that the batsman is too square on and therefore likely to play across the ball.

The temptation in trying to concentrate on a perfect sideways stance is not to allow the head to look straight down the pitch at the bowler, and so the batsman finds himself really only looking with one and a half eyes.

Both eyes should face the bowler, on a level keel with the head still. It sounds obvious, but batsmen forget that once the head moves, the rest of the body follows suit.

To sum up, make sure the feet are spread wide enough to suit you, with the knees slightly bent. Make sure both eyes are watching the bowler, *and keep that head still*.

That deals with everything, except the rather important matter of the position of the toe of the bat. It can either be grounded or not, and I change according to type of pitch conditions and the pace of the bowlers.

Assuming that I can ground it, I always do so behind my right foot. Some batsmen ground the bat away from them, but that only increases the possibility of picking it up crookedly, so I would advise against that.

The great Sir Donald Bradman apparently used to ground his bat *between his feet*. Again I would never tell a batsman to copy him because somehow the bat has to be taken outside the back foot, and

(*Left*) The face of the bat open to point, with the eyes facing the bowler and the head held still. This photo was taken as I was about to 'step into' a drive.

(*Right*) Prolific run scorer Peter Willey here demonstrates everything that is wrong in a stance – but it has not prevented him playing many fine innings over the years.

that can only be done by taking it out towards gully. But, as the record books show, 'The Don' was hardly a failure, which only proves once again that no matter how peculiar some part of your technique may look, as long as it works for you, *never change because some coach wants you to look more elegant.*

THE PICK-UP Now to the last part of the set-up before the ball arrives—the pick-up. Everything I have said so far is aimed at helping you to hold the bat properly and stand at the crease in the manner most likely to produce a straight, correct back-lift of the bat.

Remember that although this vital part of your technique can be individualistic, if a bat is picked up incorrectly, it is probable it will also be presented to the ball wrongly. I tend to take the bat back towards slip, instead of the classical takeaway back over leg stump, and in this way I adopt the same technique as some West Indians. Notably Rohan Kanhai, who although he used to pick up towards gully invariably managed to drop inside from the top and come down in a beautifully straight line.

Again, don't worry if what works for you does not suit your coach, because the game is full of players who have made the most unlikely looking methods work successfully. I have already mentioned the stances of Peter Willey and Graham Gooch. Peter stands so front-on that both feet point straight down the pitch, his left shoulder faces square leg, and it seems impossible for him ever to score on the off side. But he shuffles round just as the ball is delivered, and consequently his pick-up is not so much off line as most people think.

As for Graham Gooch, he stands sideways with the bat raised well above shoulder height, and although I think too much can go wrong from that static position, his career performances speak for themselves. Besides, both he and Peter Willey have fine records against the West Indies' fast bowlers.

Unless I am on a quick pitch and against a genuine fast bowler, I know that I tend to pick up towards the slips, and so I concentrate on whipping it into that Caribbean arc so that I bring the bat down straight.

As in golf, the important thing is to present the club or the bat square and straight to the ball through the hitting area, that is before, during and after contact.

One simple exercise will show you the perfect line of pick-up. Stand at the crease with the bat held normally in both hands. Then take away the bottom hand—right hand for right-handers—and clamp it around the other elbow. Bend that elbow 90 degrees, and the bat will be taken back towards your stumps to give you the proper line of back-lift. Remember that most players bring the bat down on the same line they take it up on, so try to cut down on the margin of error by developing a length of back-lift you can keep under control.

Don't take it back the same distance all the time, because you should vary it according to conditions. Particularly against the faster bowlers on grassy pitches—Barbados, for instance—I try to play with as little movement as possible when I first go in, and so I reduce the back-lift. Sometimes, although I don't go as far as Graham Gooch, I will stand waiting with the bat a couple of feet off the ground.

Against the slow bowlers, you can let out a notch or two because presumably you will be looking to stroke the ball around more in front of the wicket than is possible against the quicks.

Whatever your pick-up, it will work so much better if the top hand is in complete control of the bat at the beginning, and stays in charge for as long as possible during the stroke.

So many things in the stance and pick-up are

A good spread of the feet, ensuring proper balance, eyes on the ball and the back-lift in progress.

inter-related, but all are important, and none more so than the head remaining still. It is a fundamental basic in all sports to keep the head still, and yet most players forget the elementary point that once the head moves, other body movements are inevitably going to follow.

The best players I've ever seen—Allan Border, Barry Richards and Viv—keep their heads rock-like while picking up their bats and playing the ball.

The best illustration I can give is how the best use is gained from a pair of binoculars. You fix them on the target and keep as still as possible, otherwise any movement distorts the image. It is exactly the same with batting, particularly against the fast bowlers when there is just no time to remedy any basic errors made in grip, stance or back-lift.

The other thing about the position of the head is to ensure that both eyes are looking on a level plane down the pitch. I have already explained that if you don't stand sideways, the pick-up line is almost bound to go wrong.

Because it is so vital that both eyes are used properly against the faster bowlers, perhaps I'll get a little square on without disturbing the sideways structure too much. In any case, the back-lift will be shorter under those circumstances, and so there is less to go wrong.

BATS AND PROTECTIVE GEAR Just to round off my advice on the best ways of preparing for the business part of the game—when you actually have to play the ball—let me explain about the weight of bat I use and the different forms of protective gear that are now available.

Until about 1980, I used a normal weight bat, around two and a half pounds; but after trying a heavier one as an experiment, I immediately loved it and those made for me now by the Worcestershire Chairman, Duncan Fearnley, are nearly three pounds in weight.

But again, everyone should find out for themselves what is most suitable. As a general rule, most young players start off with a bat that is too heavy for them, because they are given their first bat when they are growing up.

Only try the heavy bats, therefore, when you have more or less finished your physical development. Undoubtedly, more players nowadays favour the bigger bats, and cricket has followed golf and tennis in this respect.

Racquets now have bigger heads for more power, and golf clubs are designed to hit the ball further. In the same way the bigger cricket bat is so much more destructive than the old-fashioned lightweight ones.

It is not the weight of the bat which is important: it is how balanced the pick-up is which settles which is the better bat, and sometimes I tinker around with one or two extra rubber grips to achieve a better balance.

Usually I have a couple of grips on, but although it can be one, or even on occasions three, it is very rare nowadays that I have to change one of Duncan's bats. He usually presents them to me at about an ounce or so under three pounds, and then if necessary I vary the number of grips.

At the start of an innings on a quick pitch, I will usually take out the lighter bat when I am not looking to play too many shots; so don't be afraid to change, even in the middle of an innings. Some players develop superstitions about their cricket in general and their bats in particular, but I don't go along with that.

I always believe that I can make my own luck. So if I find out any of the opposition are superstitious, I try all the harder to convince them how unlucky they are.

Regarding protective equipment, I only use either a helmet or a forearm guard if the pitch is dodgy, because in normal conditions I reckon I should never get hit if I keep both eyes on the ball. But on a pitch like, for instance, Headingley in 1987 in the Test match we lost to Pakistan, I did use an arm guard and a helmet because of the variable bounce—but that is the exception for me.

It is not because I share the view that a player's reactions are subconsciously slower if he is wearing a helmet, because the risk of serious injury is reduced. I suppose my dislike of using that sort of visible protection is the same as my good friend Viv Richards, who never ever wears a helmet. It is another way of saying to the bowler that he is not that quick or dangerous, and I will never ignore any opportunity to score a psychological point.

SUMMARY To sum up my tips on grip, stance and back-lift—anything within reason will suffice, *providing that whatever you do that is different from the normal methods, is not detrimental to your batting.*

If things start to go wrong, and a string of low scores follow, go right back and re-examine your basics. Often, a tiny little adjustment is all that is necessary, and sometimes the most unlikely people can spot it for you.

All that I have explained so far is to show how simple the game is, once a repetitive method has been found.

Plenty of power from my Duncan Fearnley custom-manufactured bat.

SECRETS OF BATTING I have repeatedly stressed so far the importance of cutting out unnecessary movement, and the time to concentrate hardest on standing absolutely still is when the ball is about to be delivered.

Some players never really think about when to start picking the bat up. They do it at the same moment in the bowler's delivery stride, whether it is a fast bowler or a spinner. Then they wonder why they are halfway through a stroke—only for the wicket-keeper to be tossing the ball back to the fast bowler. It is only common sense to quicken the pick-up against the paceman, and to wait just that bit longer against a slow bowler.

The vital difference between the average player and the good player, and the good player and the great batsman, is the apparent extra time the better players have to play their strokes. I will explain why this is not quite true, just as the theory that the great players play the ball later than other batsmen is only partly correct.

Both differences can be explained quite simply. That extra available time and the lateness of selection of stroke come because players like Viv Richards and Allan Border avoid any significant first movement of the feet when they start to pick the bat up.

If ever there is one *real secret* of batting, that is it. Even they cannot stand absolutely stock still, but whatever first movement either player makes is so small that it does not cut down his range of options to the same degree as with ordinary batsmen.

The sort of movement which is too early and too much is at the root of most batting faults, and I strongly advise the following check exercise being carried out regularly by all batsmen, no matter at what level they play the game.

At the start of a net session, ask the bowlers to help you by, without any warning, running in to bowl to you as normal but, instead of releasing the ball, to go right through with their usual action without letting the ball go. Just look at what you have done with your feet, and all will be revealed. Most Eng-

lish players tend to move their front foot forward as they pick the bat up just before the moment of delivery. This is because of our slower pitches. Conversely, the first movement of overseas cricketers tends to be either back or across their crease. This is because of the quicker nature of their pitches, and the extra bounce bowlers can obtain from the additional pace.

Next time you watch a big game, try to spot the first foot movement of the better players, and you will soon find that most English right-handers will have committed themselves to the front foot, by moving that left one at least 18 inches.

The disadvantage is obvious because they have reduced by the same distance how far on the back foot they can go, should the bowler decide the time is right to let a short one go.

This is another reason why we always struggle against the really fast bowlers, because they can only be coped with satisfactorily on the back foot. English cricket, because of its generally paceless pitches, does not produce many effective back foot players, and it never has. The number of batsmen in the last 20 years who could whack it off the back foot, are few and far between. Just think of our best batsmen in that time: Colin Cowdrey, Peter May, Tom Graveney, Kenny Barrington, Geoff Boycott, Graham Gooch, David Gower and so on.

Of course, they were good enough batsmen to cope with the short ball, and even on occasions score runs off the back foot against the real quicks. But most of them were much more fluent when driving, because that is how they learned their cricket.

The obvious exception was Ted Dexter. I didn't see much of him, but I am told that he stood stiller than most, and was equally happy to hook and cut, as well as drive. David Gower is another, although it must help that he is left-handed, and therefore playing to a different line.

Graham Gooch can also pull and cut with tremendous authority at times, but generally he looks to play forward if he can.

So try that test—have a look at where you have

Ted Dexter in full flow
with the head still and
the eyes following the
ball.

committed yourself to, and remember you've done that before you have any idea what length delivery you are trying to deal with.

The worst sort of movement with the back foot is away towards leg slip, because that destroys any real chances of getting into line against the quicker bowlers.

I will deal with these first movements again when I get on to bowling, but just remember that any thinking bowler will soon spot that first movement, and from that he can quickly sort out a player's strengths and weaknesses.

The virtues of standing as still as possible are therefore many: you give yourself the chance to move forward or back; and you will cut out that forward, half-cock defensive push at a short of a length delivery, which is the only available option if you have got on to the front foot so early.

Also by delaying your footwork, you will be more able to establish the length and play a proper stroke with authority. It is not just coincidence that the batsmen who are most difficult to contain are those who can pull and cut as well as drive.

Another big plus is that the rhythm of the pick-up is not disturbed, and providing the top hand stays in control as the bat is brought into the hitting area, any sudden late movement or lift can be better countered if you are not too committed.

I realize that against real pace, everything has to be speeded up, and I admit that I then concentrate on a first movement back and across the crease. I do this because I know that not much is going to be pitched up to me, and anyway against quality fast bowling, every batsman needs a period of adjustment to the pace and lift at the start of his innings.

But that one exception only underlines the golden rule of batting. *Stand as still as possible for as long as possible.* Put that last sentence into constant practice, and many, many more problems will be solved than created.

I set out in this book to accomplish two things. I want to explain my attitude and approach to cricket, and hope that I can open up a new area of the game to cricketers whose approach is too restricted. I want them to take the blinkers off, and although a bit of eye strain might follow at first, it won't be long before they discover just how rewarding and enjoyable the game can be.

At first it might be like that first dive into the deep end. Plenty of apprehension to begin with, but that is soon replaced by enjoyment born out of sheer exhilaration.

The other aim is to try to simplify a lot of the sort of coaching advice which has been handed down from generation to generation, without proper thought or explanation. A good illustration of this is the different guards batsmen take, and the importance of choosing the right one.

TAKING GUARD Like the points of preparation I have already gone through, I don't think that the average coach goes into enough detail about the crucial parts of batting, including which guard should be adopted and why. For instance, a leg stump guard opens up the off side, while the further over a batsman stands—i.e. middle and leg or middle—the more deliveries he will have to play straight back to the bowler or on the leg side.

I now take leg stump, although I used to take 'two leg' until I found I was getting out l.b.w. a lot. Even then the penny never dropped, until my late dear friend and coach, Kenny Barrington, suggested I might like to try a change.

Don't just pick a guard without thinking about it. Say: 'Which area do I like to play to most of all?'

As a simple guideline, top hand right-handed players should take one leg, while those players with a strong bottom hand should stand further over towards off stump.

Colin Cowdrey once took off stump in the West Indies in 1959–60 against Wes Hall & Co., simply to get himself in line, and it worked for him. This sort of willingness to adjust to change again proves the value of a batsman working things out for himself, rather than automatically accepting the word of the coach who is only going by the book.

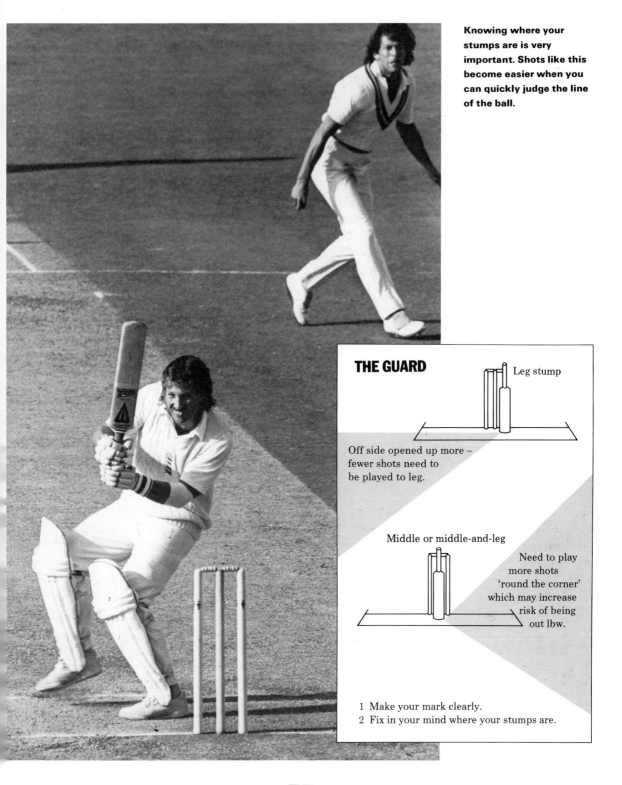

Knowing where your stumps are is very important. Shots like this become easier when you can quickly judge the line of the ball.

THE GUARD

Leg stump

Off side opened up more – fewer shots need to be played to leg.

Middle or middle-and-leg

Need to play more shots 'round the corner' which may increase risk of being out lbw.

1 Make your mark clearly.
2 Fix in your mind where your stumps are.

Sometimes, the 'book' needs re-writing, and nobody should be afraid of making up his or her own mind, no matter what the so-called experts say.

Another thing to remember, is that just because two batsmen take the same guard, does not mean that they stand in the same place. I always ground my bat behind my right foot, which means I am virtually standing on the line of leg stump. As I have explained, that gives me extra width to play to my off side strength, but other players toe their bat in some way from their foot. I don't like that because they have to move more and that is not a good thing. The whole point of a guard is to help you know where your off stump is, so that you do not play unnecessary defensive strokes at wide balls.

After all, if a ball is not going to hit the stumps, what are you defending? And of course, the wider the ball, the less of the face of the bat you are able to put to it, so either go for an attacking stroke, or leave it.

The other common fault which springs from grounding the bat away from the back foot, is that it actively encourages a crooked back-lift.

Until I started to explain the basics of preparing to face the music, I never realized how much there is to get right, and I suppose I have been lucky to find so much of what I have advised came to me naturally, without me having to think too much about it. Now I am as anxious as anyone to get the innings under way, so here we go.

PLAY TO YOUR STRENGTHS

'A guard should enable a batsman to play to his strengths, and just how well this works for me can best be seen by looking at a few run charts of my big and best innings.

'The one that reveals all is of my 118 at Old Trafford against the Australians in 1981. That innings was immeasurably a better knock than the earlier 149 at Headingley, because that was a death or glory slog in an apparently lost cause, but the Manchester innings was one I built so carefully that I only managed five singles in my first 33 deliveries.

'I then cut loose against the second new ball with 47 out of 52 off 26 deliveries, and did not take much longer to get to three figures.

'It seemed, even to me, that I had smacked the Aussies all over Old Trafford, but in fact only 18 out of my 118 came in front of the wicket on the leg side. There were two sixes, a four and two singles in that one 90-degree area.

'Run charts can be valuable, but never let them affect your natural style.'

2

THE START OF AN INNINGS AND HOW TO BUILD IT

MORE NORMAL APPROACHES So let me concentrate on more normal innings, and whether you play like me or Geoff Boycott, there are certain common factors to be taken into account.

Let me deal firstly with my own approach. It never bothers me how long I stay on nought after I have come in to bat. Some batsmen are looking to get off the mark straight away with a mid-wicket push for a single. I would rather concentrate for a few deliveries at least, to play 'in the V' as we call it—that is the area between mid on and mid off.

Viv Richards is one who loves to slide his foot forward and push a run or two through his favourite mid-wicket area, but you cannot take him as an example of too much because he is a genius. I could not do what he does and he won't try too much of what I do. We both play to our respective strengths, and that is what coaches should encourage.

When I start batting, the bowler is in between me and what I want to do, so I try to work out the best way of dominating him. Some bowlers cannot take this. They worry, try to change their natural method, and the argument is settled after a few deliveries.

Other more resilient cricketers are tougher nuts to crack. John Emburey is as good an example of this as I can quote, because he has such an unshakable faith in his own ability and method of bowling that he never gets rattled if he gets smashed around. Not that that happens too often, which is why his captains pay him the supreme compliment of entrusting the closing overs of a one-day match to him.

Somehow, I want to introduce my natural aggression into proceedings as soon possible. I keep coming back to aggression, because it is such an integral part of my game and approach, but I recognize that it takes different forms with different players. For instance, many people regarded Geoff Boycott as a run machine who ground his runs out, rather than give rein to a lot of the flair I know he had. Flair which only occasionally in one-day cricket used to be unwrapped, but I knew was always there, having travelled the world with him.

I have watched him in the nets countless times, where he has played all the shots, only to go in and revert to type. I used to think that was illogical, but he would argue it was done to get rid of his aggression before he started his innings, because he was then more likely to produce the sort of big innings needed in Test cricket.

I thought that a wrong approach, but it made him such a great runscorer, who can argue?

Whatever I have been accused of, when on the surface I have got out to a silly, irresponsible shot, nobody can ever say that I have been short of *self-belief*. I know that on my day I can destroy an attack, and turn a match right round in a short space of time. I think I am helped by batting at five or six, because the match situation has started to develop by then, and much of what I do can be viewed in that context, compared with those top order players who try to shape events.

They shape, and sometimes I try to change—there is the big difference. But I can only change things because I believe in myself, whereas there are quite a few cricketers who sell themselves short,

GOING FOR IT?

'It is only on rare occasions that I feel free to come in and go for it from the first ball. Edgbaston in 1985 against Australia was one of those, and I will never forget my first ball six off Craig McDermott.

'At 572 for 4, we were not exactly struggling, and Mike Gatting hardly needed to tell me to get on with it. But that situation was just as much a one-off as the one at Headingley four years earlier when we were 133 for 7 in the second innings, still 94 runs behind Australia.'

because they do not fully believe in themselves.

It's all a matter of courage and self-belief, with a touch of arrogance thrown in. My aggression does not come from just going in to wallop the bowling. Look back and see how many of my big scores have come when the side has been in trouble, and my initial approach had to be different.

Unless I receive some rubbish bowling to start with, I play normally for a bit longer than usual before I set out to destroy. Then I sort out their most dangerous bowler, and attack him sensibly to see if I can get him off. In those circumstances, a captain often panics and whips the bowler off, which is wrong on two counts. He just might get me out, and anyway he is still posing the same threat to my partners.

Mike Gatting did well in the 1987 World Cup on at least two occasions in this regard. Both times Eddie Hemmings was the bowler, and in matches against West Indies and India, Viv Richards and Kapil Dev had smashed him for boundaries. But Gatting kept faith, and so did Eddie, and he got both men out with well-flighted deliveries, when England were facing defeat in matches which they went on unexpectedly to win.

Such a big part of the game is who can dominate who, and no batsmen should ever settle for just going through the motions when they bat. Things rarely happen—they have to be made to, with so much depending on the match situation. If the runs are not coming, don't get bogged down—push and sprint a few singles. More likely than not, the fielders will come in and then there is a better chance of hitting a four.

A POSITIVE ATTITUDE What seems to inhibit a lot of players is if their first attacking stroke costs them

(*Right*) Attacking the bowling like this can unsettle the opposition and panic their captain into rash decisions. If it causes good bowlers to be taken off it can benefit others in your team as well as yourself.

their wicket. That never bothers me, because I am never afraid of the consequences if things go wrong. Fear has no part to play in my game. I've seen too many players start off in a team, either at county or Test level, with the sole thought of surviving to stay in the side.

My attitude is different. I go out there and tell myself, 'I've got here because of the way I play—so why change it?'

Another thing, once some batsmen get on top and start the roller coaster going, it is just as though they are afraid of how fast they might go, and they jump off. I remember sitting with Viv on the balcony at Taunton a few years ago, watching our Somerset team's approach to a fairly easy Sunday League victory target of around four runs per over. Once a four had been hit, even if the same delivery came along next ball, a different stroke was played. The attitude was 'We've got our four this over, why take chances?'

That is nonsense. Firstly it breaks your own batting rhythm; and secondly it restores some of the bowler's confidence. Not to mention helping to ruin your own side's momentum. You only have to notice how many one-day matches change right around when a side suddenly backs off when they are on

A DIFFICULT INNINGS

'Occasionally, circumstances call for the elimination of any risk, and although I find this sort of innings the hardest of all to play, I still bring all my aggression to bear, as the best way of disciplining myself. Like, for example, my innings on the last day of the Oval Test against Pakistan in 1987, when we were totally up against it, and I knew I had to stay there with Mike Gatting all day. Runs did not matter—it was just a matter of survival against their attack under the pressure of having fielders all round the bat all day, after they got that massive first innings total of 708.

'The only hope I had was to wind myself up, so that I could impose myself on them, even though it would be in a different way from usual. I said to myself: "Right, cut out all the chances of getting out, and don't play a shot."

'It was one of the most untypical innings of my life, but I actually enjoyed it more and more as the day wore on because the Pakistan side was getting increasingly frustrated with me. I concentrated on leaving alone as many balls as possible, and those I had to play, I did with bat and pad locked together—and it worked like a charm.

'We saved the game, thanks to that 150 from Mike at the other end, which shows what can be done with the right approach. In its own way I am just as proud of that effort—my slowest ever Test 50—as I am of some of the blockbusters.'

Part of my 90 for Somerset v Middlesex, NatWest semi-final, August 1983, when I played out a last-over maiden, when the scores were level, to win the match.

top. Too many batsmen think that if they try too many strokes and get out, they will be accused of a lack of responsibility.

That is negative thinking, and you'll never win anything that way. I try to keep all my 'vibes' positive, and if I can finish the match well within the prescribed number of overs, that to me is the best way of staying on top once you have the edge.

An example of that was our Sunday League match at Hereford in 1987 against Surrey, when Worcestershire won the title. Tim Curtis and I went in to bat on the slowest, lowest pitch of the season, after Surrey had managed 154, with *no fewer than 97 singles*. That illustrates just how difficult it was to get the ball away, and I know the Surrey lads fancied their chances if they could contain us early on.

They did that, because although we put on 130, the 50 did not come up until the 15th over. Then I wound up at the slow bowlers and managed a couple

of sixes, so now we were well on top and apparently cruising. There were plenty of overs left, and all ten wickets were intact, but I knew that if we just pushed around, things could so easily go wrong if we lost a couple of wickets, because nobody in the match had managed to come in and smash it around right from the start. So I kept going, but even when I got out for 80, Graeme Hick came in with the same sort of positive approach. We wanted 25 off 16 overs, but he hammered 19 in no time, and finished things off with a six to win us the match by nine wickets with 12.2 overs to spare.

We might well have won the match the other way, but that is never how I look at things.

Once I have pressed the accelerator, and I knock a few of the opposition over, I want full throttle to wipe them all out. If a side ever gets back into a match I have started to rush them out of, it is never because I have eased down in order to avoid unnecessary risks.

I am not trying to suggest that everyone should bat the way I do, because I know they couldn't. Some cricketers are not as strong as me. Neither

Graeme Hick, my partner in some classic innings, playing his favourite square drive off the front foot.

can they hit as straight, nor as hard. But they have their own strengths and they must play to them, spurred on by the right sort of *positive attitude*.

I am always on to my team mates about developing and sustaining a positive attitude. From the beginning of every match, I am trying to win; whereas some captains go the other way and aim firstly to set up a position from where they cannot lose, before they turn their attention to winning.

Sometimes in Test cricket that has to be the way to play, but five-day Test cricket is a unique form of the game, and not too many valid tactical comparisons can be made with other formats. Certainly I can think of very few three or four day championship matches where that sort of approach accomplishes anything. Fewer matches are won in the long run, and also the entertainment factor is ignored.

It is all very well county pros pleading a lack of understanding from spectators of the finer points of the game, and I know that it is mostly members and not the paying public who turn up in the week. But without those members, even in these days of wide sponsorship, the game would suffer a lot. Their entertainment must always be considered. Although the three-day crowds at New Road in the first season Graham Dilley and I had with Worcestershire in 1987 were nothing special, there was a huge increase in the membership, and I hope they agree we all gave them good value.

I know how much importance I attach to being entertained whenever I watch sport—be it golf, or football, or even cricket. That is one of the reasons why I always try to give value to the watchers.

There are so many different ways of building an innings. Geoff Boycott always aimed at ten runs a time, and in the first place never widened his horizon beyond that. I could not do that, and usually play it as I feel. For me, figure targets are bad because they inhibit me, and anyway they spoil my concentration.

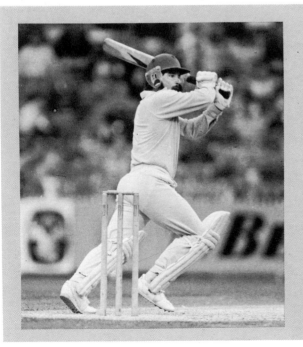

A GOOD EXAMPLE

'Just look at someone like Allan Lamb. He is my sort of cricketer because, although he has his limitations, he never dodges a situation, or ducks a challenge. In one-day cricket, he is completely different from me. He works the ball about brilliantly, taking full advantage of the lack of close fielders, and the crowd are invariably taken by surprise when they look at the scoreboard, and see how many he has chalked up without doing anything spectacular.

'Everyone remembers the 18 he took off Bruce Reid in Sydney in a World Series match in 1986. He pulled off the most astonishing win for us; but although he finished with an unbeaten 51 at a personal scoring rate of over a run per ball, he did not hit his first boundary until that final over.'

CONCENTRATION Successful batting depends so much on concentration, and I help maintain mine by switching on and off between the action. Quite often, you'll see me laughing and joking and apparently fooling around when I am batting. But as soon as the bowler runs in, I block everything and everyone out except how I am going to play that ball.

Some players cannot do that, because once they switch off, they have problems in finding the 'on' switch quickly enough. Chris Tavaré is an example of that. He keeps himself wound up by going for a walk after most deliveries. Off he'll go around the short leg area, just to think of the ball he has just faced, and to work out what he will try to do against the next one.

I get bored doing that, and so I deliberately think of all sorts of things while the bowler is going back to his mark.

Geoff Boycott is another who wound himself up tighter and tighter, and his concentration never wavered. I can't do that. He could, and there is another instance of the fascination of cricket which is played in so many different ways by different cricketers.

Early in an innings, I might keep myself geed up for a while, but I have to revert to normal pretty quickly, otherwise I find my mind becomes cluttered with things which are of no use to me at all.

Some batsmen are great chatters, and it is always important when batting for a player to take into account the make-up of his partner. Needless to say, I love to chat in the middle with the other batsman, even if it is not too much about the cricket—unless I think he is struggling and I can help him with any advice or encouragement.

It is surprising how often a batsman can lose his rhythm in the middle of an innings, and it is then his

Geoff Boycott, England v India, Second Test, Lord's, July 1979. Concentration personified; still head with eyes on the ball.

partner can help him with a quiet word, and perhaps by organizing the strike, if a particular bowler is suddenly looking dangerous.

Viv and I batted dozens of times together for Somerset, but I can hardly remember a conversation about the bowlers in all that time.

I remember one chat with Mike Gatting at The Oval when we were both just blocking for over after over against Pakistan in 1987. After yet another maiden, I met him in the middle of the pitch and said: 'Am I frightfully boring to watch?' He just cracked up, but it helped to break the tension of the situation, and I knew a laugh would not break his concentration.

A lot of players aim to bat for a session at a time, but again, while I accept that works for them, once I get time and lack of motion of that sort in my mind, it would be bound to affect the way I play, so not only do I rarely look at the clock, I am not one of those players who checks the scoreboard after every run, to see they have not been diddled.

Sometimes I look up after a while, and I am genuinely surprised to see what has happened, but I play in the way I do because various targets which fill other players' minds, never bother me.

The only time I will keep a careful regular check is towards the end of a one-day match, or in a tight finish to a three-day game, where the number of overs left is always so important.

Find out by trial and error what your mental limits are, and then evolve your own concentration key. Mine is to switch on and off, otherwise I quickly become bored and tired. Also to keep the blinkers on does not make me a better player, and I am a firm believer in not letting anything worry me more than it has to.

RUNNING BETWEEN THE WICKETS AND CALLING

There are enough ways of getting out in cricket, without being run out, and yet time and time again, the pressure of trying to sustain a victory charge produces the sort of mix-up when seasoned pros don't know whether to laugh or cry.

When most run-outs are analysed, and the blame apportioned—although there is often more disagreement about that than in deciding who was in the wrong in a car accident—it is surprising how few are unavoidable. By that I mean when the dismissal came about as a result of a magnificent piece of fielding, when it is only justice to give credit to the fielder rather than criticize the batsmen.

The other common denominator is that remarkably few run-outs happen because someone is slow moving between the wickets, rather than slow thinking.

The most important part of safe running is calling, and the understanding of that call. That in turn means knowing your partner, so that you try to anticipate everything he does. When I first opened in the 1987 Sunday League with Tim Curtis, we could both have been run out at least twice—simply because we did not know each other's habits. We soon learned, and after a while even a look and a nod was enough without any real necessity to call.

So as a general rule, get to know the batsman who, for example, often takes a couple of steps down the pitch after most front foot strokes, even though he is not looking for a run. Find out if any of your colleagues are nervous starters, and are looking at the start of their innings to get off the mark. That does not bother me because it is no big deal if I'm out for 10 or 0. My sights are set much higher than that, and if I play a big innings, I'm looking to trade more in fours and sixes than quick singles—unless of course I want to organize the strike.

But I'm well aware that my partner might be different, so I take that into account when I'm in the role of non-striker.

As long as the calling is definite, I don't think it is necessary to stick to the textbook rules which decree that the striker calls in front of the wicket and the non-striker is in charge when the ball goes behind the wicket.

If for any reason I don't fancy something I've been called for, I'll say 'No' as quickly as possible before my partner is too committed.

England v Australia, Second Test, Lord's, June 1985. David Gower brings off a brilliant reflex piece of fielding to run out Kepler Wessels.

Often when I'm on strike and I have hit one into the covers and called for a run, I have forgotten that there is danger because of a left-handed thrower and I then get sent back. That is fine—as long as it is done immediately, because the real trouble starts when the calling is either late or indecisive. This is particularly prevalent when the ball is played square of the wicket, because the two batsmen have a completely different angle of view of how close to the fielder's throwing hand the ball is.

So be prepared to share the calling responsi-

bility, and don't shelter behind the official party line that it must always be the striker's call in front of the wicket.

Also remember to keep in mind that every side has at least one fielder who is a bit special. I always mentally slot him into a 'no go' area unless it is a really safe run. Into that category come people like Derek Randall, David Gower and Roger Harper for instance who, despite their track records, can still bring off the unexpected run-out which sends the victim on his way shaking his head and feeling he has just fallen for the latest three-card trick.

Take Harper's great run-out of Gooch in the M.C.C. v. Rest of the World match in 1987 at Lord's. It was breathtaking, and yet despite Graham knowing all about the man he still got done by a couple of yards, although he never went further than five yards out of his crease.

I'm told that the great South African cover point,

Colin Bland, nailed Kenny Barrington and Jim Parks in a Lord's Test, despite the whole England side deciding they would not run to him in the covers or at mid wicket.

Calling and running depend so much on understanding your partner. My former Somerset team mates Brian Rose and Peter Denning hardly ever called after their first few innings together. A glance at each other would do, and they became just about the best pair of runners together I have ever seen. This was not just because they were pretty rapid between the wickets, but also because they both spotted a run so quickly. They would run sides ragged—the fielders would close in and suddenly, bang—four runs.

We played a one-day game at Harrogate and they actually hit something like 70 off the first nine overs with only half a dozen boundaries.

But although club cricketers and youngsters cannot expect to develop that sort of telepathic understanding because they play cricket intermittently and not on a day-to-day basis, as long as commonsense is applied, it should not take too long to work up a reasonable understanding.

Always take into account the speed of your partner. If he is a bit ponderous into his stride, allow for it, and then try to ensure to begin with that *you* are running to the danger end.

Another thing to consider is the ability of different fielders to get rid of the ball quickly. Find out those who can throw on the turn, and those who cannot. For example, if I hit one a yard either side of Chris Broad, I will take him on, but I wouldn't Tim Robinson. Chris takes just that split second longer to gather the ball and have a shy.

Although I wouldn't risk much to David Gower when he is running on to the ball because of his uncanny underarm accuracy, once he is chasing after it, I'd chance an extra run as he cannot throw quickly or hard on the turn because of shoulder trouble.

It is that sort of attention to detail which solves so many problems before they arise.

3

THE CLASSIC SHOTS

DRIVING The purists have always said that the real beauty of batting is best expressed by off-side play, and as that is my favourite area, I feel qualified to offer advice about how best to become effective and fluent there—particularly off the front foot.

I know that the orthodox coaching instruction insists that the bat and front foot must be together in playing a flowing off drive, but I don't go along with that. The real destructive cover drives are nearly always played with the bat a bit away from the front leg, in order to gain extra leverage, which in turn helps with power and placing.

I am not suggesting that the front foot should be miles away from the hitting area, because that is bound to produce a hit or miss technique, and all successful sportsmen, including good batsmen, have a technique which is repetitive because it has been tried, tested and proven over a long period. But I have seen plenty of well-coached young players stroke a nice copybook cover drive straight to a fielder, simply because they have concentrated so hard on getting the foot right to the pitch of the ball, they can't hit it very hard, and in any case they can only hit it in one place.

England v India, Third Test at The Oval, July 1982; my only Test double hundred. The left shoulder led my front foot into the perfect cover drive. My weight is going forward and the head is still. I'm pleased with this one!

The really hard hits come from a little bit of room being created in which a full wide arc of a good back-lift can be fully used. The left shoulder for the right-hander, should be the leading influence, not the foot. Anyone who queries that golden rule should just realize that you can put the front foot where you like, but the shoulder need not follow. But if the first leading movement is with that shoulder, the foot must follow unless you fall over.

England v West Indies, Third Test at Kensington Oval, Barbados, March 1981. A rare luxury of playing spin. The front leg has gone towards mid-off, although I have played the ball into the covers. The gap between bat and pad is not normally advisable.

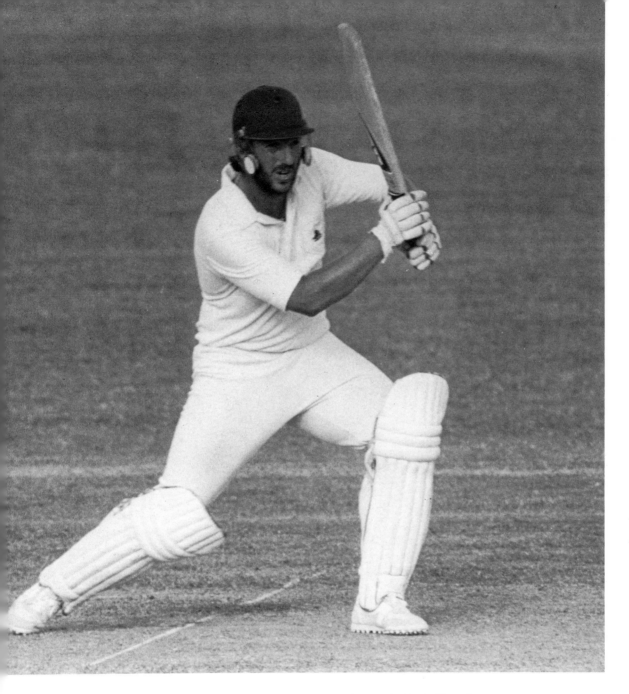

In forward play, always try to lead with the shoulder, and then the top hand will stay in control of the stroke much more easily.

The other key to a successful off drive is to ensure that you have a full and high follow through. Too many players forget about this, and as a result start decelerating the bat in the hitting area.

Golf provides yet another valid comparison here because the longest hitters are those whose exten-

sion 'through the ball' is the greatest.

Batsmen should never ignore the importance of finishing the stroke off properly, which means concentrating hard after contact has been made. That way it will be easier to place your shot, and of course to hit it harder.

Selection of the right ball to hit confuses a lot of batsmen, and this is why it is advisable to take a few minutes at the start of an innings to assess the con-

England v Pakistan, First Test at Old Trafford, June 1987. I have gone for the big one, with the top hand totally in control. It kept the blade open until impact, which increased my margin of error had the ball moved away at the last moment.

ditions. Of particular importance is the pace and bounce of the pitch. On a quicker pitch, the off drive can be played to a shorter delivery than normal, and conversely on a slow, low pitch, the ball must be that much further up.

The wider the ball, the more difficult it is to control the stroke. And naturally, the wider the ball, the fuller in length it needs to be to cover it properly.

The pace of the bowler also matters a lot, as well as what he is trying to do. Off spinners and inswing bowlers do not give you the same amount of room as the slow left arm bowler or the away swinger.

If the ball is moving or turning, then a batsman needs to take extra care with an off drive, because the swing or spin usually takes effect in the last few feet of delivery.

When I try to off drive an inswinger, I concentrate on getting my front leg a bit further over, so that I will not be 'gated'; but when I fancy a dip at an away swinger, I create a bit of room and let the top hand lead me into a full-blooded hit. The reason for this is that if I happen to get an edge, it flies harder and further, and more often than not I get away with it.

'Lucky Botham' might come from the commentator, but that is not strictly true because I have given myself the extra option, if a bit of movement induces a false stroke.

The off drive is 90 per cent top hand controlled, with the bottom hand adding a little bit of punch at the moment of impact; but try to keep that hand out of the action for as long as possible.

With the straight drive off the front foot, the bottom hand plays a slightly bigger part, and the on drive calls for an even bigger influence.

The principles are still the same. The 'other shoulder'—left for the right-hander and vice versa—should lead into the stroke with the foot fol-

This was a lofted stroke, with the front foot not having gone too far offside, which would have made me play around my front pad.

**Note the front foot
position, which has
enabled the bat to stay
perpendicular through
this on drive.**

lowing. Compared with the off drive, the foot should be alongside the pad, because the whole idea is to play the stroke with a perfectly vertical bat.

Played properly, the stroke offers the twin advantage of being played into the one area on the field directly behind the bowler's arm, where there will be no fielders, and there is quite a margin of error in the batsman's favour. If the bat is straight, any error in timing need not be fatal, because there is such a long line of contact between bat and ball, compared with, say, the pull or hook. They are cross-bat strokes and so there is just one point of contact.

A lot of batsmen find the straight drive a difficult stroke to master, because of that first front foot movement I have already talked about. If they have started to push forward too early, the front foot will probably have gone too far towards the off side to get the bat through properly.

Similarly with the on drive, which is one of the hardest strokes of all to master. I never saw Peter May bat but I gather he was a marvellous on-driver, because he was able to get the front foot out of the way so well. As a result he could play the stroke with a much straighter bat than most. Greg Chappell was another one. Also there is not too much wrong with Viv's on-side play.

The on drive whipped wide of mid on is a stroke well worth practising, and the best way to get started is for someone to stand halfway down a net and throw a few balls slowly at you in the right area around leg stump. At first, you will find that you are automatically playing *around the front leg*, so keep at it until you play *alongside it*.

All the classical strokes go along the ground according to the textbooks, and they point out quite rightly, that if you don't try to hit sixes, the chances

of getting caught are greatly reduced. I am told that Sir Don Bradman had played first-class cricket for two years before he hit his first six, and his record is the best ever.

Mine is not too bad, so I will deal with hitting in the air after the orthodox back-foot strokes which can be so devastating. Either a pull or a cut can be struck harder than anything off the front foot, because there is that much more time to set yourself, and the bottom hand can play its full part in control and power.

CUTTING The square cut is a real favourite of mine, and one which played a great part in my innings against the Aussies at Headingley and Old Trafford in 1985.

Particularly against the faster bowlers, the key to proper selectivity is width and then length. Some coaches might class that as heresy, but it is no good trying to cut a short ball if it is not wide enough; you are more likely to get away with having a crack at a better length ball, providing the bowler has given you the necessary width. The reason for this is that full leverage is essential for control, and only if a batsman can extend both arms is he able to execute the stroke properly, with the perfect control that comes from the bottom hand rolling over the top, at the moment of impact.

The body weight should go into the ball, and a tell-tale sign of a badly selected stroke is when the batsman has had to back away to leg in order to give himself room.

Of course, there are times when you can do this legitimately, but you need to be well in before you try it. After all it is extremely difficult to back away to leg, and then reverse the process just at the right time to get the body weight and the extended arms going back into the ball in unison at impact. It is like a goalkeeper going the wrong way, and then pulling off a great save. He might do it two or three times, but as a rule, he will be punished.

The classiest of all the back-foot strokes has to be the late cut. It is delicate and artistic looking, and always earns applause because it has an element of cheek in it as well.

As the name says, it is played later than any other stroke, and the same guidelines apply as with the square cut. The ball must be short and wide enough to give the batsman the chance to stay on top of the shot throughout. The square cut is normally played when the ball is about level with the batting crease, with the late cut tried when the ball is roughly level with the stumps.

The position of the back foot in both cuts is all important. *It must never point in front of the batting crease*, otherwise the body will be turned too square and an edge is the likely result. Keep the back foot parallel with the crease for the square cut, and point it towards third man for the late cut, and it will then

(**Right**) A front foot cut off a delivery, wide enough to give extensive leverage of the arms.

(**Below**) A perfect square cut; the spread of my feet has enabled my whole weight to go into the stroke, with the bottom hand ensuring that the ball goes down.

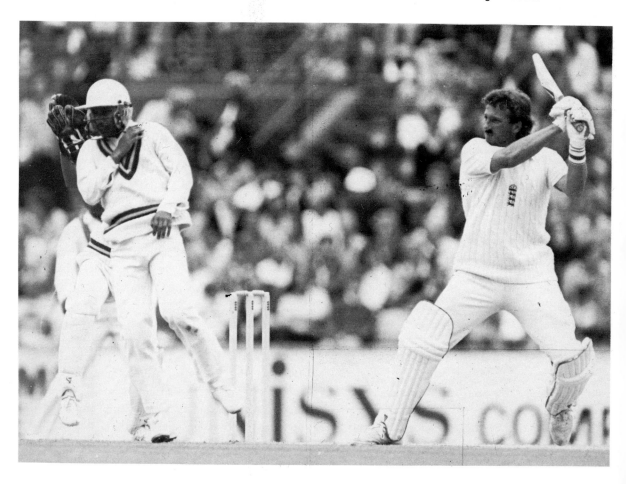

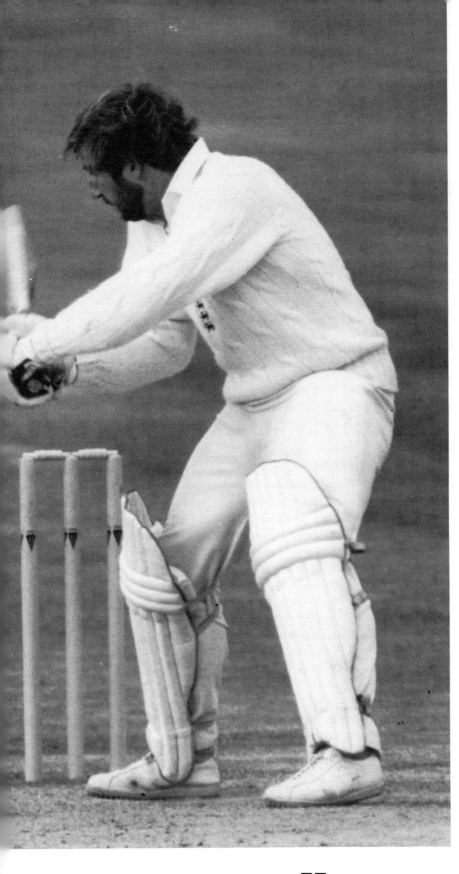

Third Test, England v
Australia, Leeds, July
1981. How to play the
late cut, with the open
blade about to hit down
over the ball. Note the
extended arms with the
bottom right hand in
control.

be easy for the bottom hand to keep the ball down, and place it where you want.

As with the off drive, be careful against the ball coming back into you from a seamer or spinner.

A batsman must be sure of himself to try either stroke against an off spinner, and it is more dangerous to try to make room against that sort of bowling than to a straight ball or one that is leaving you.

The position of the fielders must be noted, and also the pace of the pitch. So many players get out because of extra bounce, but they are not so unlucky as they think if they get a top edge, because they haven't done their homework properly.

PULLING AND HOOKING The pull and the hook are among the most exciting in the game, because they are usually played against the fast merchants and the crowd appreciates that there is quite an element of physical danger involved.

The length of the ball dictates the shot, but direction must also be taken into account. For instance,

First Test, England v Pakistan at Old Trafford, June 1987. My back foot has pivoted, bringing me to the offside of the ball and enabling my arms to extend and gain leverage. Note how my head and eyes are following the ball.

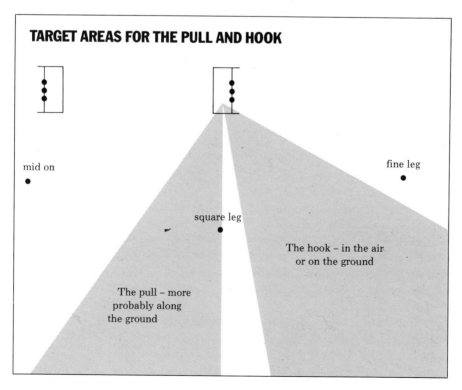

TARGET AREAS FOR THE PULL AND HOOK

mid on

fine leg

square leg

The hook – in the air or on the ground

The pull – more probably along the ground

The exciting hook shot is only possible when the basics are correct - eyes on the ball, weight properly balanced and making full use of the bat in the stroke.

although it is perfectly possible to pull a ball in front of the wicket from around or outside off stump, the same thing does not apply to the hook.

A generally accepted distinction between the two strokes is that the hook is played from square leg round to fine leg and usually goes in the air, while the pull is aimed from square leg round to mid on, and more often than not is kept on the ground—as according to the Bradman textbook.

The pull offers much more control to the batsman, providing that he chooses the right ball to play it against. The pace of the bowler determines this, because as a rule, the pull should not be played against anything over chest height.

As with the square cut, the position of the back foot and the role of the bottom hand govern everything. The foot must go across and back into the crease to give the batsman extra time to decide where he is going to hit it. Again, as with the cut, the arms must not be cramped, but fully extended in order to get maximum power. At impact, the bottom hand rolls over the top—just the same as with the cuts—with the head staying as still as possible throughout the stroke so that the eyes can be fixed on the ball until it is hit.

The badly executed pull usually comes from a cramped position which produces a mis-hit—usually a top edge.

The same principles apply to the hook, although as this is played against a shorter and higher bouncing delivery, there is much more risk involved.

The common mistake is to hook against a ball which is on the wrong line for the stroke, i.e. too wide of either leg or off stump. In the first case, a batsman can only help the ball round, and a skier to

The pull stroke keeps the ball down, with the bottom hand controlling the stroke. The greater the arms are extended, the more power there is in the stroke.

fine leg is the probable result, or even a catch to the wicket-keeper if the batsman is late on the shot. Anything pitched around off stump needs good footwork, because the act of 'fetching' the ball is fraught with all sorts of danger. A bit of extra bounce, and you cannot get inside the ball to control it. A bit of extra pace, and you are in no position to make much of a contact, and another top edge to the 'keeper is the likely outcome.

If you cannot hook naturally, forget it, because attempting it will get you into so much trouble. It is a stroke which depends more than any other on split-second accuracy of footwork and timing to keep bringing off successfully.

When hooking, the back foot is all important. Move it in the wrong direction and, even if you get away with it a couple of times, you can start checking the time of the next train back to the dressing room. It can be fatal.

Once a bowler spots a first back foot movement towards or, even worse, outside leg stump, he will exploit the weakness unmercifully.

The back foot should only ever move back and across towards the off side if a hook or pull is to be attempted against fast bowling. That way, the body is taken inside the line of ball, and if the head is still, both eyes can be fixed on the short-pitched ball until it has either been hit with the bat or avoided.

Once a flincher, always a flincher: so goes the old saying in top cricket. But although some batsmen clearly do not relish the short, fast stuff, the good player learns to cope and survive. Players like Kenny Barrington and Dennis Amiss never stood up and hooked the daylights out of bowlers like Wes

Hall and Dennis Lillee, but they *did* learn how to watch the ball and keep out of harm's way.

If a batsman's instinct is to withdraw that back foot against the bouncer, then it will take a lot of guts and hard work to cure the fault. But only when it becomes second nature to go the other way, will the player concerned gain enough confidence to go for the hook.

It is so obvious that it is too easily forgotten, that from a right hand over the wicket fast bowler, anything banged in short around off stump is almost bound to end up going down leg side, because of the angle from which it is bowled.

The odd delivery might 'hold up' off the pitch— by which I mean straighten off the seam back towards the off side—but as a general rule, any batting movement towards the leg side is only creating a physically dangerous position in which the ball will chase the batsman.

Well worth remembering is that six inches movement towards the off stump is worth 18 inches the other way. All the good hookers move the proper way and by doing that are able to sway out of the way if the ball is too quick or high to hook.

If I decide to hook, then I mentally photograph the fielders who are 'in play' for the stroke, i.e. deep fine leg, square leg and mid wicket. I note the angle they are on, and work out where I shall try to hook the bowler in question. That largely depends on his pace, and the quicker the bowler, the finer you are bound to play him. Sometimes on a decent paced pitch, if the bowler is quick enough, I don't mind taking on the man on the fine leg boundary because when I am seeing it well, I go for broke and try to hit sixes. Just as I did a couple of times in my innings against the second new ball taken by Dennis Lillee at Old Trafford in 1985. They weren't full-blooded hits, but because I had moved in the right off-side direction, I was able to see the ball most of the way and help it round.

Once the back foot has gone across, it should be pivoted upon, so that the bat can be brought through to the ball, but always be on the look-out for

Fifth Test, England v West Indies, at The Oval, August 1984; how to avoid the sudden lifter. Note the head and eyes watching the ball.

the extra bounce which will find the top edge.

It is the sort of stroke which you can stop a bit later than most—and don't hesitate to do so if there is any doubt.

Batting contains so much that is exciting, and nothing is more spectacular than watching a good hooker take on a fast bowler. It is great theatre, but never let it be forgotten that because of the physical danger element, it is also a test of the batsman's character and technique.

HITTING IN THE AIR Hitting the ball in the air is always a gamble. If it comes off, fine. The crowd cheer, your partner smiles and the bowler scowls. But the first false stroke resulting in a catch, and everything changes: the crowd barrack, your partner looks as though you have committed the original

I have gone with the ball for this hook stroke. Keeping my eyes on the ball throughout, I have been able to help it round.

(*Left*) England v Australia, Lord's, June 1985. The back foot has pulled me inside the line of ball, allowing me to pick my spot - again with arms nicely extended.

sin, and the bowler happily explains to his mates how those first three sixes he conceded were all part of a well-thought-out trap.

Let me explain why I choose to hit in the air so much, apart from the fact that a few home runs get the scoreboard moving that much quicker. I have always done it naturally—it is part of my nature to go down the pitch to break a bowler's rhythm and concentration.

It may look dare-devil, but that is not always why I do it. Perhaps the bowler is in a groove and is close to getting on top. I don't want to stand for that too long because I always aim to be in charge as soon as I can. So I do one of two things. Either I will go for an 'over the top' assault from the crease or I'll mix it with an occasional charge down the pitch as he lets the ball go.

To do it from the crease calls for a proper selection of the ball, bearing in mind the field placings. With a normal field including an orthodox mid off and mid on, I just wait until the ball is pitched up and then let go with as straight a bat as I can.

I love to hit straight, because that is the area where there are no fielders, so I force myself to think 'top hand' all the way through the stroke.

Once the bottom hand creeps in, the hit won't be straight, or as powerful, and is more likely to end up with a fielder on the leg side. It is seldom, if ever, that you will see me go for a big hit early in an innings in any other direction than straight.

The other advantage of aiming there is if I am not quite to the pitch of the ball, I can still get away with it by hitting 'through the line'. If I aim exactly straight behind the bowler, there is quite a wide margin of error for me if I drag it or push it a little. Once the fielders go deeper, then I think again and usually try to play 'inside out' over the covers.

Going for it. Guaranteed to unsettle most bowlers, the risks involved are surely worth it.

Not many players can play this stroke, and so bowlers are unused to dealing with it. The line of ball is important, but I usually give it a full go to anything around off stump against the medium pacers or the spinners.

Occasionally, when I am really going, I will even have a go over the covers off the back foot, but usually it is off the front foot that I aim for the stars.

At times I will go charging off towards the bowler, sometimes even before he lets the ball go. It is all part of my attempt to disturb him, because once he has to start to think of too many things, his concentration will waver, and then he's mine.

The first thing to work out is when to take off. If I wait until he is jumping into his delivery stride, then I know it is difficult to adjust to the sort of delivery he has in mind. Against the spinners, I can get much further down the pitch, but I need to be more careful with the wicket-keeper standing up.

The other and even more unsettling tactic to try occasionally against the faster bowlers when the 'keeper is back, is to start the charge when the bowler is still a couple of yards away from the stumps. Now he can adjust, so it becomes a guessing game. Will he assume you will keep going—in which case will he bang it in short? Do you then hope for that and get ready for the hook? Or might he double bluff and pitch it straight in at your feet?

Whatever happens, if the ball is not there to be hit, it's madness to go through with the stroke

(*Left*) **Third One Day International, England v Pakistan, Edgbaston, May 1987. The full flow of the arms enables me to hit through the line and increase my chances if I am not quite to the pitch.**

(*Right*) **This time I've 'charged' and it has paid off—during my 163 in the Silk Cut Allrounder Challenge in 1984.**

regardless. Stop the ball or let it go and regain your crease, because at least you will have succeeded in forcing a variation from him, and next time he runs in he is likely to be a bit ruffled.

But when I have got down the pitch and guessed right, the extra momentum I have got from my charge is pretty useful when I swing over the top.

I know cricket is a team game but when a ball is bowled, for that split second, it is the ultimate one-to-one situation. Both opponents are after each other, and if it is a good bowler I am up against I know I'm not going to get too many loose deliveries unless I get after him and give him something else to think about. Once he becomes rattled, then I have done a good job for the side, regardless of whether or not I go on to get a big score.

One thing I'd like to get straight: everyone seems to think that each time the ball goes in the air, that is what I meant to do. Not so. Sometimes the ball goes flying over cover when I intended to keep it on the ground, because perhaps it pitched a foot or so shorter than I thought when I decided to give it the treatment.

FOOTWORK Before I get on to how I play slow bowlers, a few comments on footwork. I have already described the best positions to get into for some specific strokes, but there are a couple of rules which never should be broken. *Just as the grip of the bat should always have both hands together, so the feet should always end up nicely apart when the stroke is played.*

Over-fussy coaching forgets that there is nothing fancy about basic footwork, particularly for strokes played from the crease. The object is to be so balanced at the point of impact that even the long, full follow through will not cause much foot movement after the ball has gone on its way.

A sure sign of incorrect foot movement is when after the ball has been played at—or missed—one or other foot has to make an extra movement to get them to where they should have been in the first place.

Watch what happens next time you see an attempted off drive fail to make contact. The batsman will probably then have to throw the front foot wider to create the missing balance. Similarly on the back foot, watch the 'fencers' who play and miss by a long way outside their off stump. Their back foot has not taken them into line, and when they stretch and miss the ball, the effort then draws the back foot into the correct place.

To gain and maintain that balance, do not fall into the trap of playing across the batting crease 'on the shuffle'. Make a good, decisive movement either forward or back, and ensure that the feet stay apart throughout the stroke.

Just think of how much variation in the length of a ball can be achieved by proper footwork—at least seven feet because you can get forward about four feet, and on the back foot use at least three of the four feet between the two creases.

When a bowler lets the ball go the distance between him and the batsman is not the widely quoted 22 yards; it is that figure *less the eight feet which is the combined distance between the creases at each end.* So 58 feet can be altered by up to seven feet which is why it is easy to appreciate the huge advantage that can be wasted by timid and indecisive footwork.

Whether going forward or back, the movement of the relevant foot is to take the batsman to the line of ball, and not away from it. Although I have so far been talking about right-handers, the same thing applies to left-handers against spin bowlers, *but not so much against the quicks.* This is because they nearly always play to a different line, which explains why so many of them appear to be vulnerable outside off stump.

To explain that: as a right-hander facing a right arm over the wicket bowler, my bat comes down

First Test, England v Australia, Headingley, June 1985. A good front foot movement has given me a perfect balance to drive over the top. Keeping the head still is vital to the stroke.

from inside to out, i.e. from about leg stump towards the line of ball delivered from over the wicket. A completely straight, perpendicular bat thus cuts down the error factor, and offers several points of contact if I happen to be early or late with the shot. This is because my line through the ball is unaltered if my top hand stays in charge. But I am much more vulnerable facing a left arm over the wicket seamer, because the ball is coming from mid on and I have to square up a little out of the sideways position in order to combat the ball being angled across me, instead of in to me.

As a right-hander, that does not happen too often, but left-handers have to deal with it most of the time. Take David Gower, or Clive Lloyd, or Alvin Kallicharran. They are all great off-side play-ers but their feet are rarely close to the bat when they off drive the fast bowlers, because the ball is leaving them all the time.

Most people fail to realize how short some of the deliveries pitch which are drivable. Again it depends upon the pace of the pitch, but on a normal strip, a good player will be looking to drive anything pitched around eight feet away from him. How can a left-hander get bat and pad to a delivery that far away which has probably pitched just outside off stump and is on its way towards the slips?

It will arrive in the hitting area about stump high and a couple of feet wide of off stump. So much of cricket is an appreciation of the angles involved and it helps a lot of players to bowl in a net on their own with no batsman there, just to see which balls hit the stumps, and where they have pitched.

Just as surprising will be the number of deliveries which miss the stumps after pitching in an area which would draw the most vehement l.b.w. appeal in the middle if a pad got in the way.

I just laugh at some of the criticism David Gower in particular gets about 'poor' or 'lazy' footwork. He knows where his strength is, and his strongest area is from mid off's right hand round to backward point. So he plays there whenever he can and as he is averaging nearer 50 than 40 in Test cricket, he can't be doing too much wrong—even if occa-sionally he gets caught at the wicket or in the slips.

David is the perfect example of how contrasting temperaments can succeed brilliantly in Test cricket. There could not be greater opposites than him and me. He is calm in appearance—I am aggressive. He is relaxed and laid back—*I am aggressive*. He rarely lofts the ball and I often do. His technical secret is that as left-handers go, he is very orthodox. I am correct, but not orthodox—and that is the big difference.

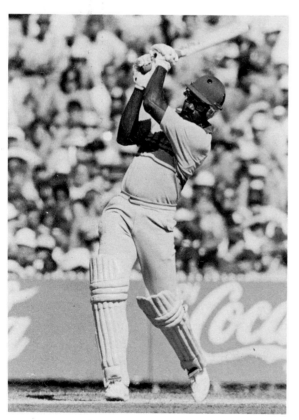

Benson and Hedges World Series Finals, Australia v West Indies, February 1985. Clive Lloyd off-drives through the ball.

4

HOW I PLAY SLOW BOWLING

The difference between how I tackle slow bowlers compared with most other players, really sums up why my approach to cricket is so different from the average. *I go out to destroy them, whereas the average player goes out to play to survive.*

I except one or two players from that comment—particularly Mike Gatting, who thinks that some spinners should not be allowed in the game.

That sort of arrogance occasionally gets both of us out, but overall, the positive approach we adopt pays off. Not only to each of us, but also to the other batsmen in the side who can go in sometimes to play against spinners whose confidence may have been badly dented.

I try to dominate them early. I suppose I face more off spinners in the modern game than any other sort of spinner, but it doesn't really bother me if long on or long off is back—or how deep anyone else is.

I wait for the right ball in the right area and if I select right, 'Bingo!', it's out of the ground. I regard that in baseball terms as 'strike one' and I aim to repeat the dose as soon as possible.

I find that with the inexperienced spinners, once I have tapped them for a couple of boundaries, they spear it in with a flat trajectory, and then it's easy.

All I have to do is to angle the bat and pick up a run a ball on either side of the wicket.

The best slow bowlers don't fall into that trap. Bishan Bedi was one who, if I managed a six off him—and I got a few over the years—would toss the next one up even slower and higher.

That is the sort of challenge someone like me finds almost impossible to duck. Vic Marks is another bowler who is never afraid of being hit. His theory is that as long as the ball is going in the air, he must have chances of a wicket.

I remember him at Lord's in 1981 against the West Indies bowling to Gordon Greenidge in the Prudential Trophy match we went on to win. When he came on to bowl, Greenidge and Desmond Haynes were going well, but Vic picked them both off in an eleven-hour spell of 2 for 44.

Gordon slogged him twice for four, but the next ball was still beautifully flighted, and 'Jake' Lever took the catch. That is what intelligent slow bowling can achieve, but so many modern off spinners really offer themselves on a plate.

Even when the ball is turning back in to me, I still try to hit straight. The times I go with the spin I never seem to hit it as hard or as far, and I got out at Trent Bridge and Edgbaston in the 1987 Texaco matches in the same way. The Pakistani off spinner, Tauseef Ahmed, tucked me up a little and in both games I was caught out on the sweep, whereas had I had the patience to wait for the chance to hit straight, I would have been better off.

Barry Richards and Alvin Kallicharran are two players I remember as being pretty special against the slow bowlers. Both used their feet well and although they did not go for the big hit too often, they were both good enough to play either with, or against, the spin.

I'm more brutal—often to my own detriment; for example, if I can hit a spinner for 20 in an over I'll do it, whereas had I been a little more subtle and taken something like 60 off 10 overs, his captain would probably have given him a longer bowl.

But I just set out to dominate, and if I do, the

NatWest semi-final,
Lord's, 1983; I hit a four
past Clive Radley.

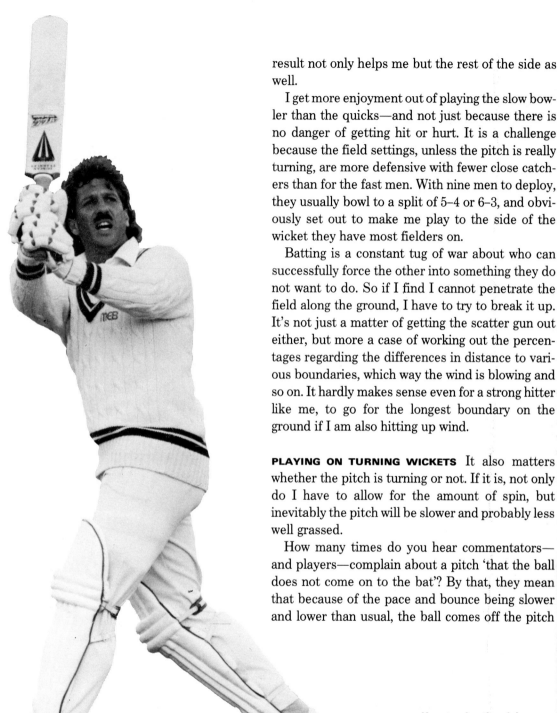

result not only helps me but the rest of the side as well.

I get more enjoyment out of playing the slow bowler than the quicks—and not just because there is no danger of getting hit or hurt. It is a challenge because the field settings, unless the pitch is really turning, are more defensive with fewer close catchers than for the fast men. With nine men to deploy, they usually bowl to a split of 5–4 or 6–3, and obviously set out to make me play to the side of the wicket they have most fielders on.

Batting is a constant tug of war about who can successfully force the other into something they do not want to do. So if I find I cannot penetrate the field along the ground, I have to try to break it up. It's not just a matter of getting the scatter gun out either, but more a case of working out the percentages regarding the differences in distance to various boundaries, which way the wind is blowing and so on. It hardly makes sense even for a strong hitter like me, to go for the longest boundary on the ground if I am also hitting up wind.

PLAYING ON TURNING WICKETS It also matters whether the pitch is turning or not. If it is, not only do I have to allow for the amount of spin, but inevitably the pitch will be slower and probably less well grassed.

How many times do you hear commentators—and players—complain about a pitch 'that the ball does not come on to the bat'? By that, they mean that because of the pace and bounce being slower and lower than usual, the ball comes off the pitch

How to play the pick-up, lofted hit to leg; weight on front foot and head upright and still, and looking for the gaps in the field.

differently, and it is much more difficult to middle a good drive.

The good players adjust their timing by trial and error, but lesser batsmen go on clubbing the ball into the ground and moaning because runs are hard to come by. Spectators can always tell when batsmen have a timing problem, when short balls are smashed straight to cover, although the intention was to hit past his left hand. The ball has not come on, and the bat is well through the stroke before contact has been made.

So if the pitch is turning, I play differently compared with a firmer surface where, even if I am not quite to the pitch of the ball, I can still hit through it.

One of the problems on a turning pitch is the number of fielders around the bat for the catch. I

I've watched this one on to the bat before driving it to the off side; placing the shot is as important as hitting the ball hard.

AN EXAMPLE

'One big innings I remember well was at Edgbaston in 1985 against Warwickshire. There was no bounce in the pitch and the grass had been taken off to help the spinners. In the second innings, I worked out the pace and bounce, and wound up against Norman Gifford and off spinner Adrian Pierson.

'I repeat some details of my innings here, just to show what can be done if someone sets out to take charge, and is successful. When I got to three figures, 94 had come in boundaries, and there were only 26 scoring strokes—one more than the all-time record.

'Slow left-arm bowler Gifford was turning it, which suited my "inside out" lofted shots, but I also managed several sixes over mid on by using my feet to get right to the pitch of the ball before I laced it against the spin.

'One of my twelve sixes caused a laugh because it went through a door at the top of the East Wing stand, and careered down five flights of steps before it reappeared at the bottom.

'My unbeaten 138 came out of 169 and I faced just 65 balls. One other thing I had thought about was the difference in distance of the boundaries at either end of the ground. The straight carry is at least 15 yards further at the City end than hitting towards the pavilion, which is why I hit most of my sixes off Gifford—although Pierson's off spin was the easier to get hold of.'

work on the theory that if they are close in, there must be plenty of open spaces somewhere, which is why I am not afraid to go for my strokes.

Once a batsman starts attacking in this way, a lot of bowlers get worried about their team mates being in danger of getting hit, and so they do not bowl as well as they can.

There is always pressure on bowlers when the pitch is helping them, because their own side thinks that they should be getting wickets, and it is surprising how easy it is to rattle the opposition with a few boundaries.

PLAYING THE SWEEP SHOT Playing in orthodox fashion against the turning ball won't bring too many runs if the bowler knows what he is doing, which is why I try to mess the field about by trying either a normal sweep, or the notorious reverse variety which seems to cause more coronaries and fits among the critics than any other stroke in the game.

I will come to that stroke last of all, but firstly a word about the 'proper' sweep after one more comment on footwork. Most textbooks and coaches are far too rigid about where the feet should be, and how to get them there. I realize that with most players, poor positioning of the feet can lead to the body and shoulders being so much out of line that a proper swing of the bat through the ball is not possible. *But* I also know a lot of batsmen who get their feet in place according to all the coaching diagrams and then find they can't hit the ball—only block it. And that is because they have ended up too close to the ball.

I agree that defensive play needs a tying in of bat and pad close enough together to stop the ball going through. But apart from the forward defensive stroke, the footwork for all other strokes should aim at one thing: getting a batsman in a balanced position to hit the ball with a free and full swing of both arms. *Make sure that your footwork gives you room.*

The orthodox sweep is a prolific source of runs if it is played properly, because once a batsman gets his eye in, it can be played almost at will against the slow bowler—irrespective of length and direction.

The whole point is to play the stroke with a horizontal bat, and not to try to hit it too hard. Against the off spinner, there are bound to be at least three leg-side fielders who will be 'in play' for any mis-hit, so concentrate always on keeping the ball down.

The stroke must be aimed from square leg round finer, depending upon where the ball pitches, but don't listen to any coach who tells you not to sweep against a straight ball. Obviously there is more risk, because of being bowled or l.b.w., but the risks can be reduced *by concentrating on sweeping to length more than width.*

Up go the arms of the purist coaches again! Let me explain why I am convinced I am right. Providing that I sweep to the right length ball, I rarely get out. And that length is far enough down the pitch for me to hit the ball with both arms at full stretch, rather than have them cramped because the ball is too far up to me. As long as I roll the bottom hand over the top at impact, it is a safe shot. The troubles start with wide deliveries, particularly those pitching outside my leg stump.

If it is an off spinner, then I can only help it on its way, rather than place it and hit it with whatever power I want. If it is turning back from leg, then either I might get a top edge, or even get bowled round my legs. This often happens with batsmen off a full-length ball which they have to play with bent arms, and it is difficult always to get your front leg in the right place to take advantage of the l.b.w. law.

If it pitches outside off stump, the problems are reversed. The off spinner is easier to hit and control, with the ball spinning in, but the slow left-arm bowler only has to straighten it a little to find the top edge.

Also of course with balls pitching on the stumps, I take into account the type of bowler and where he bowls from. An off spinner pitching around middle and leg from over the wicket, is not going to hit leg stump, so if it is the right length, that is a free hit. But a left-arm spinner only has to straighten it from middle and leg and I could be given out, so I am more careful against him when he pitches in line.

The most difficult off spinner in the world to try to sweep has to be John Emburey, because of where he bowls from. From over the wicket, he gets in so close to the stumps that often an umpire has to tell him to move away straight after delivery, because he is blocking his view from wicket to wicket.

His front foot drops in the block hole, and so a straight delivery pitching around middle stump has every chance of winning an l.b.w. decision. Also watch out for the 'arm ball' which a bowler like Embers' drifts from leg to off. Good umpires always note where a bowler lets the ball go from to help them with their decisions, and the thinking batsman should similarly treat different bowlers in different ways after studying this, and other characteristics.

If the sweep is hit too hard, then there is less control, and the ball may not even be kept on the ground. Either square leg or the man out deep behind him is there for that stroke, so don't try to hit sixes—be content with the little fish.

The more gently the stroke is played for ones and twos, the safer it is. Sometimes it is very aptly described as 'a paddle', and bowlers know they have a problem when a player can sweep safely.

Always make sure that the front leg is placed well down the pitch, to give a firm base for what is almost

The sweep shot, with the right knee bent and eyes on the ball. Note the close 'bat-pad' fielder waiting for an error.

a kneeling stroke, and remember that the bat sweeps around that leg.

THE REVERSE SWEEP The first person I ever saw play what looks such a piece of cheek was the Pakistan Test player Mushtaq Mohammed. My eyes popped at how easy it looked, and the disarray it put the bowler and his captain in. I practised it a lot to see if I could master it, and the first thing I discovered was that because there has to be a slight change of grip, *it is a premeditated stroke*.

For right-handers—and to be honest I can't think of a left-hander I have ever seen try it—the right hand has to be brought a few degrees around the handle in an anti-clockwise direction, and the left hand is loosened. This is because the bottom hand becomes the top when the bat is reversed, and governs the shot. Although there is a degree of premeditation, I work out the bowlers who are more likely to bowl a mechanical length, so that the ball is more or less going to pitch in the right area—namely outside my off stump, so that I can paddle it round and help it on its way down to third man where no slow bowler has a fielder.

To me it is a psychological shot, because once I have played it a couple of times to that deserted third man area, the bowler knows he is struggling to contain me. Suddenly he has to think of something else other than bowling to one side of the wicket on a length. Now he has to worry about moving a fielder to discourage the stroke, and that in turn leaves a gap somewhere else.

This is why I don't view it only as a source of runs, but also as an unsettling effect on the bowler which often brings indirect benefits. I think this is the counter-argument to the view that 'why bother with a shot with so little margin of error if you can play so well with orthodox strokes?'

The first time I ever did it without thinking of the consequences was in a Lord's Test. I got away with it and I made 108 against Pakistan in 1978. I think it is a legitimate stroke which we'll be seeing more and more, particularly in one-day cricket, where the fields for spinners are so defensive, and usually packed on one side of the wicket.

In one way it is less risky than the orthodox sweep, because it is played when there is no fielder behind the wicket on the off side for the catch. This is possibly why Mike Gatting made a mistake in the 1987 World Cup Final in Calcutta against Allan Border, because there was a fielder there. He also got a deflection off his shoulder, but that was probably because the ball was pitched too far to leg.

Hark at me giving 'Gatt' stick, when I've resisted any attempt to make me cut the stroke out.

Although I wasn't in Madras when Mike got his 207, I know that he whistled through the 190s with several reverse sweeps against Ravi Shastri who was trying to close him down by bowling his slow left-arm stuff from over the wicket to seven fielders on the leg side.

With only two to beat on the off side, Mike really was given a free hit, and as he particularly wanted a double hundred with Chairman of the England selectors, Peter May, watching, he clearly did not think he was taking too big a risk.

Gordon Greenidge pulled it off with great success at least a dozen times in his 122 at Lord's in 1987 for M.C.C. against the Rest of the World. He did it mostly against Roger Harper's off spin, but he even managed to 'do' Abdul Qadir a couple of times.

Compared with the 'proper' sweep, you cannot hit the reverse one very hard, so instead just concentrate on laying bat on ball. With virtually no chance of giving a catch, providing that the right ball is chosen, the risk element is minimal.

To sum up, people are wrong who say 'Don't play it because it is not worth the risk.' I think I have shown how little risk there is, and anyway it helps me to get the fielders where the bowler does not want them. That is what I am always trying to do, and time and time again, the reverse sweep has helped me do it.

There are other ways of doing this, and so I now want to describe a few of the more unorthodox strokes, and why I try them.

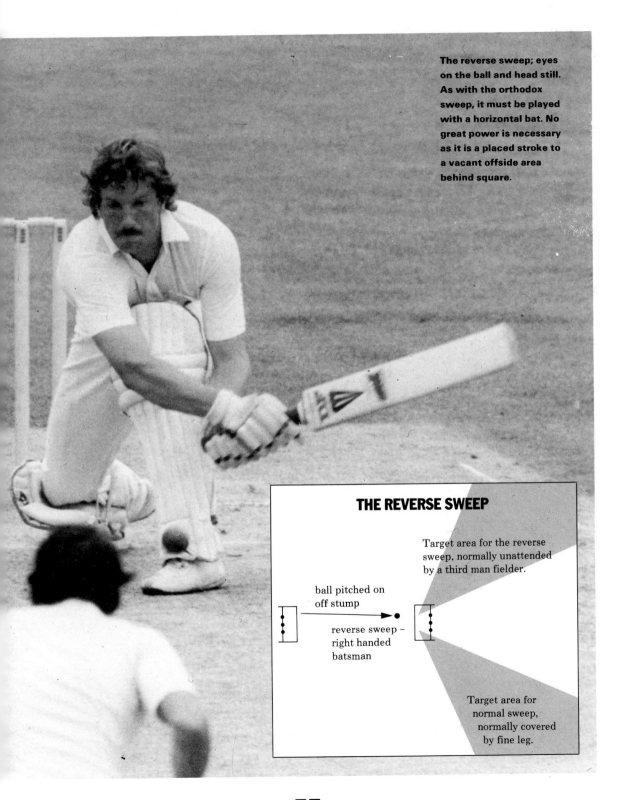

The reverse sweep; eyes
on the ball and head still.
As with the orthodox
sweep, it must be played
with a horizontal bat. No
great power is necessary
as it is a placed stroke to
a vacant offside area
behind square.

THE REVERSE SWEEP

Target area for the reverse
sweep, normally unattended
by a third man fielder.

ball pitched on
off stump

reverse sweep –
right handed
batsman

Target area for
normal sweep,
normally covered
by fine leg.

A BAD EXAMPLE

'I know I was done at Old Trafford by Greg Matthews in a Texaco one-day match against Australia in 1985, but he out-thought me, and I had no real complaints. I had hit him for two sixes—one a real big one—and I thought he'd be bound to fire it in. He didn't, and diddled me easily by lobbing it up and I was through with the stroke before it hit my leg stump.'

5

UNORTHODOX STROKES

Over the years I have developed a few strokes which seem unorthodox, but really they are only extensions of more correct looking strokes in which my grip, stance and back-lift stand me in good stead.

Because my natural method is so basically correct, I find it quite easy to try strokes which might look outrageous, but in fact the percentages are quite good. For instance, the lofted hit over the covers or slips, off either front or back foot.

THE 'INSIDE OUT' COVER DRIVE Let us take the airborne cover drive to start with. Once I have weighed up the pace and bounce of the pitch and my timing is working, if the field placings are normal, it is one of the safest shots imaginable. Mid off, cover point and perhaps extra cover are usually in an arc about 25 or 30 yards away from the bat, and so I wait for a delivery with enough width which is quite well

How to play 'inside out', by the left hand keeping the blade open through impact. Not all my weight has gone on to the front foot; this enables me to hit the ball in the air.

Viv at work, in this case driving along the ground during the Old Trafford Test, 1988.

THE MAESTRO

'I remember Viv Richards playing two of the most spectacular hits with an inside-out stroke I have ever seen during his record-breaking, 56-ball hundred against England in the second innings of the Antigua Test match in 1986.

'He shaped to make room to John Emburey, then before he bowled, feinted to move back to the off side, and it was a real game of bluff and counter-bluff.

' "Embers" guessed right by anticipating Viv going outside leg stump to try to find the big gaps past cover point, and fired in an ankle-high full toss which would have missed leg stump by quite a bit. But Viv kept the "inside out" arc going so brilliantly, even against this medium pace low full toss, that he actually hit it over Neil Foster at long off for an astonishing six.

'Neil was on the boundary, and was about the tallest player on the field, yet it was comfortably over him for a carry which was later measured as being around 90 yards.

'If we thought that was something, it took about five minutes for the maestro to bring off a huge hit off yours truly, bowling at the other end trying for the one wicket I needed then to overtake Dennis Lillee's record aggregate of 355 Test wickets. I knew what Viv was after, but I still could not help giving him the perfect ball to give the full works to—a wide, slightly short of a length delivery outside off stump.

'The left foot went down about middle and off, and the top hand took him through the ball with terrific power. The boundary rope was 75 yards from the middle of the pitch, and ten yards behind that was a double-decker stand.

'The second tier was about 15 feet up, and the ball went ten rows back, so I reckon that was a carry over wide long off of at least 135 yards.'

pitched up, although it does not have to be a half volley.

It needs to be wider than the ball from which the ordinary off-side drive along the ground is played, but why most players find it a difficult thing to try, is because their bottom hand comes into play too early. As a result, the top hand and arm are not fully extended, and at impact, the blade of the bat is starting to close. The result is either a mis-hit, or a stroke played with no real power or timing.

I have stressed the importance of my 'inside out' technique, and it governs the whole of this shot. I concentrate on keeping the full blade of the bat coming down from around leg stump in an arc which takes it out towards cover point. I make the left arm lead the whole way until, just before I hit the ball, the right hand then imparts extra power. After all, the whole point is to clear the in-field, and so the harder I hit it, the more likely I am to succeed. Because I am playing quite a lot away from my front foot, it is really playing across the line, which is why the ball sometimes flies square or even behind point down to third man.

If the ball is really wide, my follow through is often over my right shoulder instead of the left one, because that is how hard I try to stay 'inside out' until I have smashed the ball. I cannot control the placing, but it is such a destructive stroke that the rewards outweigh the risk element.

SQUARE CUT AND UPPER CUT When you decide to hit in the air on the off side, let the top hand lead for as long as possible, *and don't hold anything back*. It must be as full-blooded a stroke as you can play.

Off the back foot, I often try a square cut in the air which is actually more of a slash, and on occasions, I will even go for the upper cut over slips if there is no third man.

The square cut is best played at a rising ball, and because the bottom hand does not roll over at impact, as with the normal stroke, there is much more power available from the full extension of both arms. That is the real key to the whole shot, so you must have the necessary width of delivery, before you try it.

As for the upper cut, the faster the bowler, the more likely you are to clear the fielders, but because it is more of an edged stroke there is much more risk with it, so make sure the game situation will allow it before you try it.

Some players—Graham Gooch is one—won't hold back if the fast bowlers surround them with close catchers; and Kepler Wessels is another. They believe that there are plenty of runs on offer, providing the strokes are positive and not tentative.

Not many coaches are keen on these sort of strokes, but I think every player should realize what effect a few out of the ordinary shots can have on the bowler.

RIGHT OR WRONG COACHING I don't believe that the usual coaching of young players is flexible enough, particularly with regard to unorthodox strokes. Coaching should always be based on common sense, and this should take into account the particular strengths and weaknesses of the individual concerned.

The wrong sort of unimaginative coaching will stifle rather than encourage young talent. Good coaching is the maximum use of someone's ability. Only basic errors should be altered. What I believe should come first with kids, is to let them hit the ball a few times and then work out how best to help.

I am told that Ted Dexter went to see 1400 black kids have their first introduction to cricket in the Atteridgeville township near Pretoria in South Africa. About 60 black and white cricket coaches split the kids up into groups of about 30, and then paired them off to let the kids, who were all under 12, find out what it was like to catch a ball.

Then the basic bowling action was shown them, and finally the magical cricket bats were produced, and the grip and stance demonstrated. Ted was very taken up with the whole concept, until the coaches tried to get the kids playing their first stroke with a bat, and to his dismay, the stroke

coached into them was the *forward defensive push*.

He had a word with the organizers of what was an exciting project, and offered his opinion that it would be a much better idea to tell the kids to let the bat swing through and hit the ball. From that beginning, it would be easier to get the lads to throttle back into the defensive stroke, rather than the other way round.

It is actually the same theory as getting budding spin bowlers to spin it as much as they can, before they concentrate on line and length. This is because if accuracy is concentrated upon first, whatever grip is used disappears once the lad tries to impart extra spin—but more of that later.

I am nearly at the end of the batting section of this book, and I have suddenly realized that is the first real reference I have made to defensive techniques. This has not been done deliberately, but I just set out to try to describe my attitude towards batting, and to show how most of my technique is actually correct.

It is fair to say that my success has come because of my technique and not in spite of it. But at times, even I have to play defensively, so let me finish with a few tips which I think we'll find are not too dissimilar from those I have given about the rest of batting.

An airborne, off-side, cut. As with other potentially risky shots, check where the fielders are and hit the ball hard.

6

DEFENSIVE BATTING

A straight bat is the key to defence, and that comes from a strong top hand. For right-handers, the left hand should dominate their forward defensive play, because that can angle the bat where it can best combat the turning ball and kill the spin.

I really am proud of a few of my innings when, for the sake of the side, I have had to concentrate exclusively on defence. I have already referred to my Oval innings against Pakistan in 1987, and I also remember with pleasure a time when I spent 90 minutes getting just six runs at Sydney. I concentrated on shortening the back-lift a little, and always playing with my bat and front pad together.

That way, if the ball spins back in to me, I reduce the chances of giving a catch to short leg, because the 'sucker' dismissal is for a batsman to push out too far in front of his leg, and any inside edge can go straight to short leg. Also by pushing too firmly, a catch can often be given somewhere else.

If the ball turns the other way, providing that the top hand is relaxed and keeping the bottom hand out of the action, then there is some chance of ensuring that an edge does not carry to slip. If you are going to play defensively, don't go looking for the ball—let it come on to you.

There was no better batsman in this respect than Geoff Boycott, and all the great players have the ability, when necessary, to play defensively and adjust to sudden late movement or spin.

Against the faster bowlers, back foot defence

comes more into play, and the real secret here *is to stay in the sideways position. This can best be accomplished by keeping the back foot parallel to the batting crease.* Once it points towards cover, the whole body has to square up and the bat is bound to be brought down across the line of ball.

Use that back foot to keep the bat straight on the down swing, and also use it to get in line. That way, if the ball suddenly bounces, there is a much better chance of fending it down by taking the bottom hand away and letting the top hand relax the whole bat.

Why the West Indies' fast bowlers are so successful is that they force batsmen on to the back foot in no-man's-land, where they can only fend away from their bodies and give catches behind the wicket.

Getting right in line helps a lot, although I remember one occasion when doing just that cost me my wicket. It was at Lord's in 1987 against Wasim Akram, although it was probably his left-handed angle of attack which did me. He got me in such trouble when he was bowling from the Pavilion end, because I failed to pick up the delivery quickly enough and because I was right behind it, when it suddenly threatened my throat, I could only fend off a simple catch.

I can think of a few batsmen who would have got away with it, because they would not have been in line, but despite that, I do know that the real success of back foot play is to use it to get behind, and not away from the line of ball.

Also make sure that whether against spin or seam, when you go back, you use the crease as much as possible. Not by playing across the line, but by making a definite foot movement. That way, you get extra time and distance in which to play the ball, and that counts for a lot.

Fifth Test, England v West Indies at The Oval, August 1984. Because my top hand is in control it has dropped the bat below a ferocious lifter, and my relaxed right hand grip has released the bat and kept me out of trouble.

Against the spinner, you can watch the turn off the pitch, and decide whether to play it or not; and against the fast ball, the extra yard you have given yourself could make all the difference between surviving and getting out.

Also remember that when the team needs a

Lance Gibbs, West Indies, about to bowl over the wicket. The wide spread of the forefinger and second finger can be clearly seen.

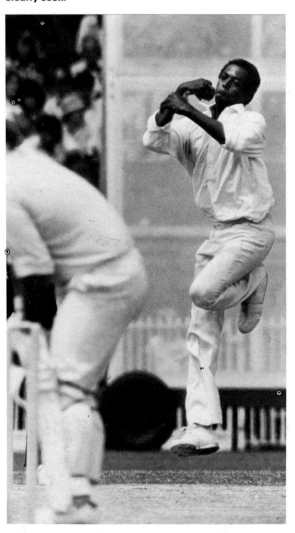

defensive innings, the more deliveries you can leave alone the better. Work out your line of off and leg stump and use all the protections of the l.b.w. law.

The other advantage of leaving alone a number of deliveries is that this puts the bowler under pressure from his captain, and shows that you are winning the battle.

Particularly against off spinners, the good defensive player tries to play in to the turn as much as possible—thus negating the strong leg-side field. He does this by letting the top hand lead the dead-bat defensive stroke on a line from leg stump out towards mid off or even extra cover. Providing the bat is kept behind the front pad, the short legs won't get a sniff, and the off spinner will then have to try something else—like switching to round the wicket to create another angle.

It is surprising how many of the game's great off spinners did not like going round the wicket, and therefore were not so effective when they had to switch. Lance Gibbs and Hugh Tayfield were just two instances, and they got nearly 500 Test wickets between them.

Once an off spinner does go round the wicket, then usually the batsman has to play more deliveries. But the principle of playing behind the front pad is just as important, as is the role of the top hand.

Remember that a defensive technique is not necessarily a passive one. The idea is to unsettle the bowler, and although it is harder to do when runs are not important, it can still be done by frustrating his normal method of attack so that he is forced to try something different.

I really do enjoy the occasional defensive battle, but as is no real secret, a lot of my pleasure comes from winding the opposition up. I am undoubtedly happiest when I can give full rein to my natural attacking talents.

The more people who develop a similar attitude, the less likely it will be that matches will peter out to an expected draw—some amazing results can be snatched from the fire.

PART

THREE

1

BOWLING TECHNIQUES— AN INTRODUCTION

ATTITUDES They say that you can tell a lot about the character and temperament of a bowler by his technique and approach, and I suppose I am no exception.

For most of my career so far, all I have been interested in when I was given the ball, was to take wickets. Containment never occurred to me as a worthwhile tactic, because I reckon the best way to restrict the scoring rate is to get a few batsmen back in the dressing room. So I have been prepared to take risks and gamble with all sorts of unlikely deliveries to that end. A long time ago, I gave up counting the number of times the word 'lucky' was used about one of my performances.

If I had taken a few wickets, each dismissal would be analysed and the usual view was that 'golden arm' had struck again with an erratic mixture of long hops and half volleys.

And yet I carry on getting people out, so I must be doing something right.

What few people realize—opposing batsmen and the media in particular—is that I am always thinking about how best to tackle different batsmen, and believe it or not, I reckon I have thought out quite a large proportion of my wickets.

I admit that my attitude towards bowling is the same as batting—and fielding, come to think of it. Namely, attack and be aggressive as often as possible. Make things happen—just do not sit back and let a game drift along.

Look at the leading wicket-takers in Test cricket: Richard Hadlee, Dennis Lillee, Imran Khan, Bob Willis, Kapil Dev, Fred Trueman and so on. How many times do you think when they were given the ball, they just trotted in and went through the motions until their spell was over?

It is not coincidence that the most prolific wicket-takers are the most aggressive, and I like to believe that although there might have been better bowlers than me, *there has been none as aggressive.*

From the time I was first really encouraged with the ball by Tom Cartwright, I wanted to find out more and more. I could always swing the ball away, so I wanted to learn the other one. At school I was always in the game because I could shine in every department, but it niggled me that when I went on the Lord's Ground Staff, nobody ever took my bowling that seriously. Yet there I was, a strong lad who was keen to bowl and could at least move the ball around.

Although I did not realize it until I started to listen to Tom Cartwright when I went back to Taunton, I must have had a good hand action. As I hope to explain, *a correct hand action is a must if a bowler wants to be a consistent wicket-taker.*

The coaching textbooks can go on for as long as they like about a sideways action. They can hammer home for ever the value of sighting the batsmen inside the leading front arm in order to pull you round, and they can also try to prove that the position of the feet sets up the rest of the action.

I do not go along with that, because like the hitting area in cricket and golf, all the preliminaries count for nothing unless the vital part is in place at the right time. In batting that is when the hitting area is entered, before, during and after impact; and with bowling, it is *when the ball is released*.

Where I do agree with the coaching manuals is that with the great majority of youngsters, where they place their feet in the delivery stride is likely to control the position of the body, and the position of the body is likely to control the all important hand action. But only *likely to*; not *bound to*, as my great mentor Tom Cartwright proved in one of the greatest medium pace careers in post-war English county cricket. In the decade of the sixties, he got over 1000 wickets in nine years for Warwickshire with the old ball. He taught himself to bowl every known variation of seam and swing, by working out for himself what to do with his bowling hand and when best to use a particular delivery.

More of that and him later. Before that, let me explain my attitude towards batsmen.

Each one I bowl against becomes my worst enemy until I can turn him into a nice chap by watching him walk back to the pavilion. I know most of the players in the game and how they like to play, but it does not take long to assess a newcomer.

Watch how he holds the bat—hands apart as we have already worked out, means a strong bottom hand, so he probably prefers to cut, pull and generally favour the leg side. Tie his grip in with his stance, and try to spot the first foot movement as your arm is coming over. That soon tells me whether he prefers to drive or not, and it is only a matter of concentration before I can slot him away into the memory bank.

What is worth remembering is that sometimes it pays to bowl to a batsman's particular strength instead of his weakness. If he knows that you are trying to exploit the latter, he is likely to be extra careful, and so you get nowhere; but as soon as he is fed his favourite stroke, his ears go back, and he can't resist it.

Again, that is a matter of learning about what makes each batsman tick, but even my critics will agree that I have psyched a few players out in this way, by mixing things up so that they become unsettled and apprehensive.

Look at the Australian Andrew Hilditch. Even though he knew what I was after, I bounced him out three times in the 1985 series, and although I have wasted a lot of runs against other players in trying the same thing, I have never minded conceding a few boundaries in trying for wickets.

The modern Test match is pretty difficult to win, and wickets are always at a premium, which is why I don't mind finishing with 3 or 4—or better still, 5—for 100 off about 30 overs rather than 1 for 60 off the same number.

I know which is better for the side, which is why, just as I am not afraid to drop a few short, I am never scared about pitching a full length in an attempt to force an error.

As I shall go on to explain, if conditions favour swing bowling, the dangerous delivery is the one that is pitched further up than normal because the longer the ball is in the air, the greater the chance for it to swing. And move off the seam as well for that matter. That is because the different trajectory of a fuller pitched up ball compared with the one that is dug in enables the ball to be in contact with the pitch a split second longer—even from a fast bowler—and so the seam has the extra chance to 'bite' and move the ball.

I always try to keep my captain in touch with what I am trying to do, so that he won't lose patience if I am getting smacked about. I soon realized that I can't take wickets standing at slip at both ends, which is why I love to bowl long spells. A few captains have been criticized because it seemed that they couldn't get the ball off me, but that was only because I had convinced them of what I truly believed myself. Namely, that I could get a particular player out, if I could carry on bowling.

In top cricket, strike rate is the most telling figure of all, and I have taken a wicket for England every 54 deliveries—compared with 53 by Bob Willis and 50 by Fred Trueman—so I think that is the answer to critics who say that I am lucky, or wasteful, or both.

But I do not have to justify my bowling—I want to pass on some of the things I found so helpful.

A perfect example of 100% aggression; a good body rock action has pulled me into a full follow-through. Also my head has stayed still which helps rhythm and hostility: one sniff of a return catch and I am there.

Back to the basics, which is how best to develop the best hand action to suit a particular bowler. Firstly, work out what is your best natural pace. It is easy to settle into a medium pace groove, always bowling well within yourself, but you must be more adventurous than that.

One or two people saw me as an out and out fast bowler, but Tom Cartwright always insisted that I had something which was of more value in a different way. I could 'hit the deck' with my natural action, and so many of my wickets have come when I have got the ball on to the batsman that bit quicker than he had anticipated.

I love to charge in, and some of my most memorable spells have come when I have got well and truly wound up, and in return, so have the crowd. I feed off them so much. Just how much they can lift me is shown by my 5 for 1 spell at Edgbaston in 1981 when Australia only wanted 151 to win.

Team mates reckon they can always tell when I am in a rhythm, because I bounce in to the wicket, rather than come in with a more laboured run-up. That is what aggression can produce sometimes, and although I reckon there are plenty of better bowlers who have played international cricket and got less wickets than me, I also believe that had they possessed less talent but more drive, they would have achieved more.

When I finally quit cricket, I shall be a happy man in one respect, because I know that particularly with the ball, I always pushed myself right to the limit. No matter what sort of cricketer you are, you can have no regrets about your level of performance, providing that *you can look yourself in the eye and know that you have always given your all, and never let your head drop.*

I think that is even more important for a bowler than a batsman, because one mistake or flinching error with the bat, and someone else takes his place. But if things go wrong with the ball, the bowler has to keep going, because anyway there are fewer bowlers in a side than batsmen, and there isn't much of a hiding place.

That is why I am proud of the fact that I caused many more problems with Mike Brearley and David Gower by wanting to stay on, even when I was being whacked about, than I would have done had I said: 'No, it doesn't look as though it is my day, forget me and try someone else.' This happened, for instance, at Edgbaston, against the Aussies in 1981 when I asked to bowl when the game looked lost. Suddenly I clicked and we won by 29 runs.

I have always believed that I could get anyone out at any time—even someone like Viv—and I don't care if sometimes I was wrong and it cost the odd match. I have won a few games that looked lost or drawn, and any cricketer would rather win and lose five matches out of ten than draw eight and win either one or two.

That is why I think I have always got more satisfaction out of bowling than batting, because I am the attacker. I have never been afraid to experiment with different pace deliveries, or from round the wicket as a variation. The plus factor of that is that an angle is created which occasionally produces a catch behind the wicket, but of course I know that my chances of bowling a player, or getting him l.b.w. are considerably reduced.

I never like to see a settled batsman, and even if he has played a couple of maidens from me, I never mind tossing up a half volley to see if I can make him commit an error.

So much of cricket is played in the mind, particularly with bowling, and with Test cricket played on pitches prepared to last five days, it is as much my attitude and approach, as technique, which has brought about my success.

The slower you bowl, the more control there is over the hand action, but what any good seamer must find out, is his optimum pace at which he is still in charge when he releases the ball.

BASICS—THE GRIP *Nobody else can advise you about that first vital factor.* Do it by trial and error, and to show yourself what control you still have at different speeds, chalk up one side of the ball, or

My natural aggressive
appeal.

there are practice balls on the market which are white on one side and red on the other.

With a normal seamer's grip—the first two fingers on either side of the seam and the thumb underneath—the whole idea is to release the ball in such a way that it goes through the air with the seam in an upright position.

That sounds elementary, but it is surprising how many first-class cricketers have not worked out which way the ball revolves when it leaves the hand.

Think about it. The last part of the bowling hand to leave the ball is . . . ? Right, the tips of the two fingers, which brush down behind the ball, and therefore *the ball should be revolving gently backwards in its own vertical axis.*

Tell that to quite a number of cricketers, and they will look at you as though they have just been told that the moon is made of green cheese; but once a bowler appreciates that, he has taken the first step towards appreciating the art of seam bowling.

And it is an art, done properly. Make no mistake about that. There are so many variations a seam bowler can teach himself, once he has mastered the correct grip.

Having worked out the best natural pace at which a bowler can still let the ball go in an upright position, the next thing to work out is how tightly the ball should be held. Richard Hadlee is a prime example of a great bowler who holds the ball loosely, right at the end of the tips of fingers and thumb. That works for him because he has been able to develop such marvellous control with a loose grip.

I need to hold it tighter, and therefore more of the fingers and thumb are on the ball until I let it go. The trap to avoid here is to make sure that even though you hold it tighter, the two fingers still brush down the back of the ball and not across it. If that happens, then the ball rotates through the air from side to side, and the chances of it swinging or hitting the seam, which is the whole idea, become less and less.

Some good fast bowlers hold the ball well back

GRIPPING THE BALL — THE SEAM BOWLER

Ball revolving backwards

Ball released by bowler – the fingers brushing down the ball

The basic grip – batsman's view

The basic grip – the side on view

1 Get the basic grip right first.
2 Work on variations later.

into the fingers. Greg Thomas is one, but I am sure that he would improve by leaps and bounds if only he could learn the knack of not 'throttling the ball'.

It is amazing how many common denominators there are in golf, batting and bowling. In each case, the grip should be firm but not tight. Once brute strength takes over, then rhythm is lost and invariably effectiveness suffers.

I cannot stress too strongly the importance of *getting the grip right*. In batting, things can work despite individual variations, but in seam bowling, if the grip is wrong, there is no chance at all of being a good bowler.

SWING BOWLING The next thing to find out is what sort of natural bowler you are. I was always an away swing bowler, but the average beginner moves the ball back in to the right-handed batsman. This is because it is easier to obtain that sort of movement—the chest-on action is the rule rather than the exception.

It is much harder for a natural inswinger to learn the outswinger, than the other way round, for the following reasons.

I have already explained that the hand action governs everything, but with most youngsters, where they place their feet leads on to a correct body action, which in turn produces a good hand action. But I have seen too many coaches slavishly and needlessly force a lad to get his leading shoulder round by dropping his back foot parallel to the bowling crease, and positioning his front foot towards fine leg.

It is a good sounding theory, but having got back into the correct position before delivery, a too early unwind still produces a hand action with which the ball is let go with the seam pointing towards fine leg, i.e. an inswinger.

And the other way around, I have seen a bowler arrive at the wicket apparently too square on to do anything but push the ball in to the batsman, but still contrive to let the ball go with the seam angled towards first slip and thus produce the perfect away

swinger. That is the importance of individuality.

My Worcestershire team mate Phil Newport is the perfect example of this, because he has learned to master the hand action for inswinger and outswinger with no change of body action. Even his own team mates cannot pick any difference.

Now I don't pretend that I have given that much thought to my bowling, but having learned how to swing the ball both ways, my extra pace made me quite a handful when conditions were suitable.

The other basic of swing bowling is the obvious one of which way the shine faces. I know that a new ball is shiny on both sides, which in fact is why sometimes it does not swing as much as a slightly older one which has been worked on for a few overs. By that time, the shine has been maintained on one side only in order to produce the two contrasting surfaces which engineer the swing. Make sure that you liaise with the other bowler, as to which side you are both looking after, but as a general rule, concentrate on the side with least printing on.

The theory of swing bowling is that the ball moves in the air from the opposite direction of the smooth side, because the less resistance on that side from the air pushes the ball the other way; i.e. for the right-handed bowler, if the bowler holds the shine towards the leg side, an away swinger will follow and with the shine facing the off side, an inswinger is the result. Always providing, of course, that the ball maintains its upright position from the hand on to the pitch.

Often in a match, it is a puzzle why the ball starts to swing—or more likely stops. So much depends upon humidity and the dampness of the pitch, and believe it or not, some balls swing more than others.

Successful swing bowling depends on so many delicate, and at times indefinable factors, which is why a bowler should never be afraid to experiment. By that I mean, conditions may look tailor-made for swing bowling, and yet the ball goes straight. It just could be that your hand action has slipped the odd degree out of true, so if everything else fails, adjust the angle of the seam a bit either way until you find

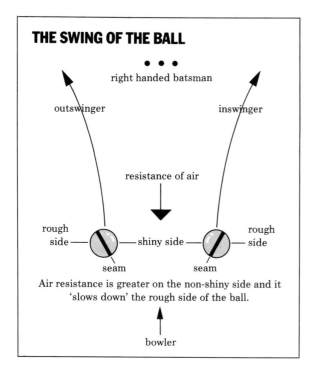

THE SWING OF THE BALL

• • •

right handed batsman

outswinger   inswinger

resistance of air

rough   rough
side — shiny side — side

seam   seam

Air resistance is greater on the non-shiny side and it
'slows down' the rough side of the ball.

bowler

out exactly what will work on the day. It varies, of course, otherwise cricket would just be a mechanical game—and it certainly is not that.

Another trap to avoid is that, having learned to move the ball in the air both ways, remember that it is virtually impossible to set a field for both the away swinger and the other one. Use the one as your stock ball, and the other as a variation, but *do not try to attack equally with both.*

The away swinger was the basis of my best performances, particularly my 8 for 34 against Pakistan at Lord's in 1978. Sometimes, when everything clicks into place, a bowler feels he has the ball on a piece of string, and that was one such day for me. I got the right line and length from which the ball darted away at the last moment, and that doesn't happen too often. The most frustrating thing for an away swing bowler is when he can move it away from off stump or outside, but when he adjusts towards middle stump, the ball will not move.

The inswinger never gets that trouble because it is so much more a natural movement and there is

much more width outside off stump from which the ball will still swing.

Apparently, one of the great post-war inswing bowlers, Cliff Gladwin of Derbyshire, actually used to go around the wicket sometimes when the ball was doing a lot—just like the off spinner will switch when he is getting a lot of turn, in order to create a more dangerous angle.

Mike Procter was another, and I remember him getting a hat-trick from round the wicket at Southampton against Hampshire in a one-day game, and he nailed his great friend Barry Richards as one of the three wickets.

I really believe that there are no limits to what a bowler can do, whereas the same cannot be said about batting.

There is so much to bowling and how you tackle each batsman. When there is anything in the wicket, I like to think that I can attack, but just because little is happening is no reason to give up. That is when I turn to trying anything in an effort to get a wicket and thus create pressure on the new, and even settled, batsman.

I will use the whole width of the crease, and sometimes alter my action in an attempt to shake the batsman's concentration. One favourite ploy of mine is to deliver a ball à la Jeff Thomson—sling fashion—with my bowling arm kept well hidden behind my back.

I try to avoid falling into a routine pattern, because if I do, I get bored anyway.

Cricket offers so many challenges, if you look for them, and if you take each one on, it adds so much to your enjoyment and involvement in the game. Sometimes I get it wrong, but it is never for want of trying. One example was in the 2nd Test against the West Indies at Trinidad in 1986, when I talked myself into the new ball, thinking I could bounce out Gordon Greenidge and Desmond Haynes. My first five overs went for 39 and I handed the initiative to Viv's side, but at least I did it for a reason. Whatever the critics might have said, I *did not* just charge in and let it go.

MY CHIEF MENTOR

'Back to Tom Cartwright here. He started off as a net bowler, and firstly taught himself to swing the ball both ways. Having done that, he bowled at a genuine medium pace, and so he decided to work on the other subtleties which might confuse the better players.

'Having worked out how to deliver both the away and inswinger from close to the wicket and wide out respectively, he reversed the pattern against the more observant batsmen who watched his point of delivery.

'He then moved on from that, once those players were ready for that ploy. He realized that they were watching his feet, and so learned the art of positioning them one way, and then bowling the other one. That is, he would drop the back foot parallel to the crease, and let go an inswinger, or would arrive at the wicket more square on, only to get his wrist cocked in the right way to produce the away swinger.'

Every innings provides different conditions, and never think that what you did once, can be repeated automatically. The pitch may be slower, or your natural rhythm may vary so that you may have to adjust your length. The shine might not last as long, and so you have to resort to trying to 'fiddle' a wicket; and there is no way of knowing this until you are out there bowling.

The big message of this introduction to bowling techniques is *never take anything for granted and always be prepared to experiment.*

BASICS—THE WRIST I have deliberately concentrated first and foremost on the bowling hand action, because without it nothing will happen, no matter how perfect a bowling action a young bowler may have coached into him.

Before I go on to other basics, let me deal fully with the wrist action. It really is the part of the hand action which controls the position of the seam. A correct wrist action will maintain that control, whereas a sloppy one will waste most of the good work already done.

All the great attacking bowlers *have their bowling wrist cocked and behind the ball at the moment of release*. There it is, one of the few golden rules in bowling which, if broken, cannot be put right. By 'cocked' I mean that as the bowling hand goes back the wrist should be bent away from the batsman, and that position should be held as long as possible as the bowling arm and hand come over into the delivery swing.

The advantage of this is that the bowler can then let the ball go with a whip-like flick of the wrist. When his timing is right, that produces unexpected

England v Australia, Third Test, Adelaide, December 1982. The bowling hand and wrist are nicely cocked away from the batsman, ready to 'whip' the ball through.

'nip' off the pitch, which is the dividing line between the ordinary bowler and one with that extra bit of devil in him.

The wrist is really the support of the bowling hand, and the position of both dictate whether that seam will go through the air upright or not. What happens to a bowler who lets the ball go with the wrist above the ball, is that he immediately loses a good yard of pace, and also squeezes the ball out with the seam likely to go all over the place.

Try this test for yourself. Hold your bowling arm out straight in front of you, with the wrist completely in line with the hand. Now bend the wrist back, and you will see how it should be positioned just before delivery. It should be cocked and ready for action.

So that you can see the obvious advantages, bend the wrist the other way, so that the fingers point to the ground. It is impossible to release the ball properly that way, yet so many bowlers use that method and then wonder why everything happens in slow motion.

THE BOWLING ARM The higher the arm, the more bounce and lift you will get, but if your natural action is lower, don't try to change it, whatever the well-meaning coaches tell you. It will have compensatory qualities—like skidding the ball on to the batsman on a quick pitch for instance. Jeff Thomson is one prime example of that who, from not too short a length, would be at the throat.

That is a prime example of making the best of what nature gave you, which is why my tips will be general ones, rather than the normal ones of 'get your left shoulder round, and concentrate on getting the feet right'.

Where would someone like Mike Procter have been if a coach had got hold of him as a kid, and ironed out all the obvious technical faults in his action? The very open-chestedness and that peculiar delayed front foot action which gave the illusion that he was bowling off the wrong foot, were two of the reasons for his outstanding success.

The textbooks say that a good fast bowler should rock well back in his delivery stride to wind up a body coil which generates real pace. Admittedly in my earlier Test days that was the principle I worked on, but there have been plenty of great fast bowlers who ran straight through the crease without any of the body-rock mentioned above.

Apart from Procter, Malcolm Marshall is another, which only proves one thing: that real pace, like a knock-out punch from a boxer, is a gift. If it isn't naturally there, it cannot be manufactured.

Too much is said and written about a body action, but what really controls it is the head. *Keep your head still throughout the delivery stride*, and you won't have to worry about much else.

If the still head keeps the eyes looking down the pitch, then a great deal of unnecessary movement of different parts of the body will be avoided. I always concentrate on keeping my head still above all else, because I know then I am more collected at the crease and able to try different variations without having to strive for rhythm.

(*Left*) Worcester v Kent at Worcester, April 1985. Hand action for the inswinger, with the seam angled towards fine leg, the supporting thumb underneath and to my left of the seam.

(*Right*) Back foot turning me into a good sideways position. Note the upright head position which helps maintain a correct delivery.

(*Left*) Everything ready for the outswinger: the leading leg is on its way towards leg stump, the wrist is cocked with the first two fingers astride the upright seam; my eyes are fixed on the batsman.

(*Right*) England v Australia at Headingley, 1981. Looking at batsman on left side of elbow, ensuring the left hip produces a good rotation through the delivery stride.

(*Left*) England v Australia, Third Test at Leeds, July 1981. Start of the unwind, with the left side holding its position nicely. If it collapses, the bowling hand is forced into pushing the ball in at the batsman.

(*Right*) The moment of delivery, with the left side rotating through and over the front leg. The left foot is pointing at fine leg, preventing too early an unwind.

(*Left*) Second Test, England v West Indies at Lord's, June/July 1984. Even though the right foot is coming past the front one, the head position still enables me to watch the ball on to the bat.

(*Right*) One-and-a-half strides on from the previous picture and the head position is still held.

ORTHODOX BASICS FOR FAST BOWLERS Some fast bowlers might find the orthodox basics of help to them, so here they are.

Find out what is a comfortable run up to the wicket. Too many bowlers run too far, and apart from slowing the game down unnecessarily, an over-long run destroys rhythm and balance.

Gradual acceleration should be aimed at, so that forward momentum is at its greatest in the last few strides. If it comes naturally, jump on to the back foot, turning sideways in mid-air. Try to bang the front leg down towards leg slip, and hold that sideways position as long as possible from the start of the body action to the finish.

A straight front leg is the ideal, because that achieves two things: it helps a bowler use all his height, and the braced leg gives maximum resistance to bowl against, which in turn means extra pace and nip.

Try to develop a nice width of delivery stride. If, at the moment of release, the feet are too far apart or too close together, balance will suffer. A too-pronounced spread will lead to a no-ball fault, and too close together will mean that your body is through before the ball is released.

For a right-handed bowler, the front left arm is important. Wherever that leads, the rest of the body must follow. So ensure that it pulls you down the pitch and not away towards the off side too early. Once the upper body unwinds, a chest-on action is inevitable; while, as I have explained, that is not necessarily a bad thing, it can lead to bad habits.

The position of my feet has opened out a little over the years, so that I am now a bit more square on. Even in my best time for England, although I used plenty of body in my action, I have never been in the classic mould. Quite often I also did not bowl with a completely braced left knee, but still I have managed to hurry up a few players over the years. Which really proves what I have said earlier—bowling is so basically natural that a bowler can do all sorts of things which the average coach will frown on, and yet the results will come.

Even more so than batting, be natural.

(Left) The ball has gone, but the head has not. Keeping the head still and level throughout the delivery stride is essential to obtain rhythm and accuracy.

(Right) Second Test, England v Australia at Brisbane, December 1982. A rare spell of off spinners – bracing the left leg helps maintain a good body action.

VARIATIONS Most of the successful Test bowlers had something out of the ordinary, and I reckon my main quality is that I have always been able to sustain long, hostile spells in which I am always trying to unsettle the batsmen.

At the start of a new spell, it always takes a little while to settle down. A new rhythm has to be found, and also whether or not the ball is moving about. If it is, then the variations to be tried are far fewer than on a flat track when the ball is going straight through.

Take a situation when the ball is swinging a lot, and I have got a good shine going and there is a favourable cross wind. The away swinger is going nicely, and so I am bowling to several slips and gullies. If a particular batsman starts to settle down, the big temptation is to slip him the inswinger, but that isn't always the best variation, because as like as not he will pick the change of action, and I will have few fielders on the leg side anyway.

What I sometimes do is simply to run up as though I am going to bowl another away swinger, *but I reverse the shine*. So with the same away swing action which has moved the previous deliveries away in the air, I then produce a straight ball, which can often induce a false stroke.

The best variations are the smaller ones—not the obvious sort which can be spotted a mile away. A good and well-disguised variation of pace is another unsettling thing for a batsman to combat. By that I don't necessarily mean the much slower ball, but rather one just a little slower or quicker than the others.

I am told that a lot of my wickets have come when I have suddenly put a little more into a delivery, which has hurried on to the batsman, and either 'gloved' him or hit high on the bat as he has gone for a pull or hook.

'Lucky Botham' is the cry, but it is rarely true. One of my strengths is my physical strength, and I can generate that extra half a yard without any appreciable extra effort, more readily than most bowlers.

A general criticism of my bowling is that I overdo the bouncer, but you will rarely see me try it when the conditions allow for swing or movement off the seam.

I have explained how important the hand and wrist action is in this department, and if there is movement available, it usually pays to reduce pace just a little, in order to retain the maximum amount of hand control.

Also don't forget to keep the ball pitched up, and don't be afraid to invite the drive. I often deliberately offer a near half volley, after I have taken mid off away, so that the batsman will be tempted into a drive he would not try with a fielder there. The point is that he is taking a chance, because the further up the ball pitches the more it is likely to move, and once he is committed to the shot, the wicket-keeper and slips are in with a chance of a catch.

Always take careful note of the way each batsman stands at the crease, because if he is in an unusual position to start with, then there are some things he just cannot do. For instance, young Ejaz Ahmed of Pakistan started off his Test career with such a closed stance that the immensely promising right-hander would stand at the crease with his left foot about six inches further over to the off side than his back foot. This automatically drew his body round that way so much that the left shoulder pointed at mid off, instead of straight back towards me, the bowler.

Obviously he ran into trouble around his leg stump, and in the Edgbaston Test in 1987, in their second innings, I concentrated on trying to pitch the ball somewhere around middle and leg, and then move it from leg to off. That is just about the hardest ball in the book for a seamer to bowl, but I managed it a couple of times. The first time, I was sure I had him l.b.w., but the decision went his way.

Still I kept at it, and in the same over I pitched one even further over towards leg stump. He played round his front leg and missed, and to my great pleasure, back went the leg stump. Bowled behind his legs—that does not happen too often in top

THE BLUFF

'One instance of the ordinary bluff working was when I captained England in Barbados in 1984, and Viv Richards came in to bat. Graham Dilley was bowling, and we made quite a show of getting our fine leg in the right position.

'Viv watched and took due note, but "Dill" did him with a well-pitched-up ball around off stump. My great friend edged a catch to me at second slip, and it was our one high spot of a tragic game—the one during which Kenny Barrington died—to see Viv on his way for a very rare duck.'

cricket, but it was a particularly satisfying dismissal, as I had planned and worked hard for it.

Anyone who stands open—the other way with the left shoulder pointing towards mid on—is a candidate for the outswinger pitched around middle and off, because he is bound to be playing across the line.

I always try to bowl what I guess the batsman wants to receive least of all. Work on that principle, and you can't go far wrong.

Often I will let a couple of bouncers go, just to unsettle the batsman and get him looking for it. Sometimes I will do it when I have nobody out deep at fine leg, because I reckon the temptation to hook will then be almost irresistible. I then try to bounce him from a bit further up, so that it is not high enough for him to help it on its way over the in-field. I am after a top edge or a gloved edge to the wicket-keeper, and I have taken a few wickets that way.

Good direction is much more important when the pitch is doing something than when it is not. I always try to make the batsman play if I am moving it, and my usual line is on or around off stump. That is known as an overseas line, because on their pitches where there is less movement than in England, bowlers learn to bowl where they can best force an error, when the batsman is looking for off-side runs.

Bowling on good batting pitches is a different thing altogether. Then I am prepared to experiment, and sometimes I will deliberately bowl several wide ones, hoping to break the batsman's concentration. If he leaves them, he is not making any progress; if he has a crack at them, I might have a chance of getting him out.

Similarly, I will sometimes set a couple of men out deep for the hook, much to the annoyance of the pundits. I think it is a legitimate tactic, whether or not the batsman relishes the hook.

The hook is the most difficult stroke to control, and I don't mind giving away a few boundaries if I can buy a wicket this way. The other thing, of course, is that you can make a great fuss of setting

your deep leg-side field with the utmost accuracy, so that the whole crowd is waiting for the bouncer. Then slip in the yorker, or to get really complicated, if you think the batsman is waiting for that because you have been too obvious, still give him the bouncer.

MORE ON ATTITUDE My aggression is never far from the surface, but a lot of people misunderstand my target if they see or hear me getting wound up after a catch has been dropped off me, or I have been hit for four. Or on some occasions when I have had an appeal turned down. Admittedly I have been known to bemoan my lack of luck, but most of my apparent spite is directed against myself—or perhaps the batsman—but not the umpire or the fielder.

I have dropped enough catches in my time to know how badly anyone feels as soon as one hits the deck. Naturally, as a bowler I am disappointed, but I work on the safe theory that it was not done on purpose, and the longer I stay upset, the less effective I will be with the ball.

As for umpires, I might have a word with those I get on best with at the end of the over, but there is just no point in getting his back up by showing obvious dissent. I know I have been hauled up for one incident in the 1985 Trent Bridge Test match, but most of the umpires around the world will back me up when I say that I am never any trouble to them.

I have even gone out of my way in team talks before a Test match, to hammer home the sheer stupidity of taking the umpires on, because in the long run it is bound to rebound against anyone who does.

Different bowlers like to bowl different ways on good batting pitches. My chief mentor, Tom

First Test, England v Australia at Headingley, June 1985 – a good unsettling bouncer.

Cartwright, used to get meaner and meaner, and give the batsman absolutely nothing in an effort to frustrate him and force an error.

My approach is the opposite. 'Here it is. Come and get it.' So a few runs have gone west! But what best to do under different conditions, is up to each bowler to work out for himself. The textbooks can never teach that.

I have mentioned the importance of shining the ball, and towards the end of a long, tiring spell, fielders can help by polishing it on its way back to the bowler.

Even when I am bowling with a slow bowler, I expect him to give it a rub, because I depend so much on that for movement. The other thing a slow bowler should remember is that if he rushes through an over too quickly, he is not being fair to the pace bowler at the other end. I am not asking him to slow things down unduly, but even an extra 30 seconds can help the other bowler to collect himself for another six deliveries.

I am often asked about my attitude towards tail-enders. Simple. Get into them as early as possible. I know some of the old-timers frown on roughing up a lower-order batsman, but all I can say is that in their day, there used to be a lot of real rabbit batsmen coming in lower down. Nowadays, almost without exception, they can all play a bit, and if I lay off them early on, I am not doing the best thing for my side because the longer they stay, the more difficult they are to dislodge.

Of course, I would not bounce someone who cannot defend himself—the Australian Jim Higgs, for example—but if he was hanging around for more than a few minutes, I would gently remind him how kind I was being in pitching them up.

SWITCHING STYLES I have dealt exclusively with bowling seam up, but occasionally new ball bowlers will part their fingers to lay one or other against the seam to cut the ball off the pitch. It really is an attempt at a fast off-break or leg-break, but the pitch needs to be receptive to spin before it works.

Make sure you practise it in the nets first because that sort of delivery is so difficult to control at pace, as the hand action is different from the normal one used by seamers.

I have mentioned variation of pace, and a useful tip for bowling a slower ball with little change of action, is to push the ball right to the back of the fingers. Remember I said at the start of this bowling section that the nearer to the tips of the fingers the ball is held, the more pace and snap will be generated. So it is only logical that if it is held tighter, the ball must come out of the hand slower.

SWITCHING TO THE CARTWRIGHT STYLE I have often been asked just how difficult it was for me in Australia in 1986–87 to switch my bowling style completely for the second part of the tour. What forced the change was the tearing of muscles in the rib area of my left side, which I did during the second Test match in Perth at the end of November.

This is an injury all pace bowlers dread, because no matter how fit you are, there is no way of ensuring it never happens, and once it has, only time and rest bring a recovery.

Contrary to what most people think, it does not happen for the right-handed bowler when he is stretching back in the delivery stride, before he uncoils and lets the ball go. It happens either as, or immediately after, the ball is released, and the left side is contracting as the body weight comes over and through the left leg. That violent rotation sometimes 'nips' a rib cartilage, and the result is a searing pain—just as though a red hot needle has been jabbed in.

Why it is unavoidable is that, unlike most other muscular injuries, it does not happen when a bowler is comparatively 'cold' at the start of a spell. More often than not it strikes in the middle of a long bowl when every muscle is warm and well-stretched, and I suppose the ultimate cause of it is an extra few degrees of that body rotation.

There has hardly been a bowler who has not suffered it at least once, but it was the first time I had ever sustained it during that Perth Test match.

As people are always telling me, I never do things in moderation, and my injury was such a bad one, that for well over a week I could not even breathe without a terrible pain. The England physiotherapist, Laurie Brown, tried to tell me to be patient, but all I wanted to do was to get fit before the third Test, which was due to start in Adelaide a couple of weeks later. I kept telling people I would be all right, but because of the lack of any significant improvement in the next ten days, I knew deep down I had no chance of getting myself fit.

It scared me a bit at first, until I spoke to a couple of ex-players in the travelling English media corps, and as they knew what I was going through, they were able to reassure me that, although it would be a slow process, time would eventually put things right. But patience is hardly one of my strengths, and so I fretted from day to day, hoping each morning when I woke up that a miracle would have happened and the awful pain would have disappeared as quickly as it came.

Because my injury was so severe, I could not even play in Adelaide as a batsman—as Mike Gatting wanted. The day before the game, Mickey Stewart took me on to the outfield of the famous Adelaide Oval, to throw me a few balls for me to stroke around with the bat. A couple of forward defensive shots were enough, and the indestructible 'Both' had had enough.

The next couple of weeks brought about sufficient improvement for me to play in the Melbourne Test, where I bowled a bit at very gentle pace and still picked up five wickets. Although I did not miss another game on the tour, the injury did not finally clear until the following June, which is why I'll never be impatient about an injury again.

I have gone into such detail about the first serious injury I ever had because that is why I switched my style of bowling to one of medium pace containment. Even though I had no choice, it did not prove as difficult to come to terms with as I originally thought it might.

I have already said that I have always looked for challenges in life and cricket, and that attitude helped me no end. I realized that I just could not bowl properly, as I understood the word, for several weeks; so either I played in the rest of the series and the following one-day internationals as a batsman only, or I changed my style completely to get through as a support bowler.

In its own way, to come to terms with that was one of the biggest challenges I have ever overcome. What helped me was that once I had settled into a rhythm in a match, I could bowl for much longer spells, although I would get frustrated occasionally if a batsman was taking root and I could not have a go at blasting him out.

Actually it was not the first time I had adopted this role, because I did it for Somerset a couple of times the previous August, when I returned to first-class cricket after my nine weeks' suspension. In one innings at Leicester I actually bowled 43 overs to take my 6 for 125, and I found a different sort of satisfaction in 'fiddling' my wickets.

I soon found out it was only a different sort of thinking that was necessary, and as I have always thought a lot about what I try to do with the ball, that was no hardship.

Similarly in the Melbourne Test, when to general amazement among the England team as well as the media I trotted in to bowl still feeling the side injury, although by this time it was manageable, and still managed to split the ten Australian wickets with Gladstone Small.

As Geoff Marsh and Allan Border were among my five victims, and I managed three slip catches as well, I was pleasantly surprised that I could pull my weight at that level of cricket, despite only being able to operate at half throttle.

Before I go on to give a few tips about medium pace bowling, one more word about the challenge involved. Too many cricketers accept their fate without trying to change it. That is not for me, which is why I was so determined to make a success of something so foreign to my nature.

How I approached the problem was to tell myself that I would show the disbelievers that the fiery, aggressive madman could actually get people out in a gentler way.

By the time the Perth Challenge and the World Series one-day games came along, I had developed my new style so well, that on several occasions I was England's most economical bowler. Also, because I could not reasonably be expected to bowl at the end of the innings, due to my lack of pace when the real stick was flying about, I was used as first or second change, and usually bowled my 11 overs straight off.

Obviously the slower a seamer bowls, the more accurate he must be, because any straying away from line and length will be punished unmercifully. I soon discovered that because I had always had a good, still head position throughout my career, I could easily settle into a groove.

The real problems arise when the head falls away before the ball is released, and takes the body with it. As a result, the bowling arm is being pulled out of line and has to find direction and length all on its own.

If the head stays still, with the eyes fixed on the target, the front, non-bowling arm can lead the body and bowling arm down towards the batsman into a directional groove. Bowling that way is like launching a wheel on a smooth, vertical path.

I mentioned the target, and here again, that is something to be worked out individually. Ask many bowlers what they look at when they bowl, and they just do not know. There can only be two target areas, and often they can be combined. Some bowlers like to look at where they are trying to pitch the ball, while others concentrate on the batsman.

I find it possible to incorporate both areas into one, because even though I may be looking at the length I am aiming at, the batsman's feet are still in my view, and so I can see if he proposes to pre-determine a particular stroke, such as either giving me the charge, or backing away to leg, so that he can try to force me through the off side.

With slower seam bowling, it is so important to keep watching the batsman, trying to spot any movement towards a pre-determined shot.

My eyes are firmly fixed
on the batsman as I get
ready for the release.

Just after delivery and I
am still watching the
batsman.

The advantage of the full
follow-through perfectly
demonstrated by this
diving catch off my own
bowling; Fourth Test,
England v Pakistan, July
1987.

2

FIELD PLACINGS

It is especially important for the medium pacer to know as much as he can about the way each batsman likes to play, because for much of the time he will be trying to frustrate him with containment. Only when the ball is moving about regularly should the medium pacer have an attacking field. A couple of slips and a gully will normally be enough, with the other six fielders deployed to make run getting as hard as possible.

I find that on the average-paced pitch, an orthodox third man is not so necessary as he is for the faster bowler because the edges will not go so fine or so quickly. Instead I use him as one of a ring of at least three on the off side, who are all saving the single. That leaves me three fielders for the leg side, and again, sometimes a fine leg is not necessary if I am bowling a good line. It is best to have him back at the start, because if I do stray towards leg stump, it is a free hit over the in-field. Once a long spell is being developed, the bowler should be confident of his ability to bowl on or around off stump, and so the deep fine leg can be brought up backward of square leg to save the single, in line with ordinary mid wicket and mid on.

If the pitch is untrustworthy, a forward short leg can be useful in more than one way: he can pick up a bat–pad catch, or a catch off the glove or splice if a ball unexpectedly lifts; but just by standing there, he can also worry a batsman into being reluctant to get on to the front foot as much as he should. Then

the bowler can pitch it that little bit further up, which in turn gives a slightly better chance of something happening off the pitch or in the air.

CONCENTRATION Genuine medium-paced bowling has to be worked at constantly, and demands just as much concentration as slow bowling. Tom Cartwright's fine career proved this. When he started off in the Warwickshire side in the fifties, he was really a specialist batsman who was good enough to score a double hundred. Then as he started to bowl more and more, he found that because he had to develop concentration with the ball, he could no longer sustain it for long periods when he batted. By the time he came to Somerset in 1970, he had dropped to number eight or nine, and finished off his career even lower.

Of course, all bowling needs concentration, but for the fast and fast medium performers, they have a greater margin of error in their favour because of their extra pace.

The first thing to establish when first you bowl in a match, is the pace of the pitch and therefore the length area for you. That can vary from bowler to bowler, even two of the same pace. One of them may come right over the top and hit the pitch with a good body action, whereas someone else will be more round arm, and so the ball comes off the pitch at a different height.

The great Hampshire medium pacer, Derek Shackleton, used to infuriate one or two of the other bowlers in the side, particularly on wet pitches. By sheer accuracy, he would create his own helpful spot on the pitch, by knocking the top off in the small area in which he invariably pitched the ball. Having done that, he would be able to get more lift and movement than anyone else. Even when they succeeded in bowling from his end, they would have difficulty in hitting the right place, because it was not their own normal length area.

There is one trap to avoid—the one of having settled into a nice groove of line and length, then to forget about trying a few subtle variations. I make no

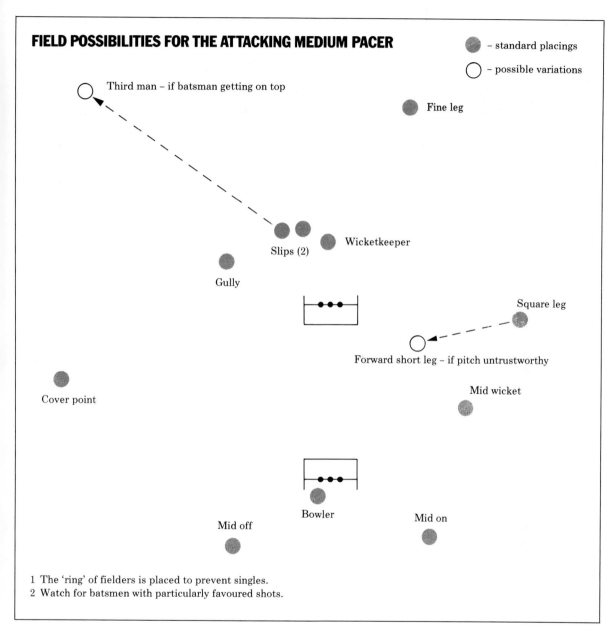

FIELD POSSIBILITIES FOR THE ATTACKING MEDIUM PACER

- standard placings
- possible variations

Third man – if batsman getting on top

Fine leg

Slips (2)

Wicketkeeper

Gully

Square leg

Forward short leg – if pitch untrustworthy

Cover point

Mid wicket

Bowler

Mid off

Mid on

1 The 'ring' of fielders is placed to prevent singles.
2 Watch for batsmen with particularly favoured shots.

apology for keeping on coming back to Tom Cartwright, because he taught me more than anyone else, and I still ring him up for a bit of advice, if I think something needs sorting out.

He was unjustly accused of being too mechanical in his bowling, but that was not true. When another bowler followed him at a particular end, he would find several different foot marks across the entire width of the bowling crease.

Too many bowlers say, 'I can only bowl from one place, because it feels uncomfortable to let it go from a different place.' That view is rubbish, and just another case of settling for one level of performance, without even trying to see how much improvement there is available if they bother to look for it.

As a general rule, the wider a bowler's ordinary point of delivery, the less effective he will be, because he is automatically cutting down his chances of hitting the wickets or gaining l.b.w. decisions. But, as with most of the advice I have given in this book, enough individuals have been successful from wide out to prove once more the stupidity of trying to push everyone into the same mould.

The West Indian, Colin Croft, is the perfect example of a bowler who made it at Test level with a technique that would have been frowned on by the average coach, who would have tried to alter his bowling action. Colin would run in straight, and then in the last couple of strides veer away towards the extreme edge of the return crease. The left foot would be splayed out even further in the delivery stride, until sometimes the batsman would think the ball was being bowled at him from mid off.

I saw good England players in the West Indies in 1981 drawn into playing at balls outside their off stump which were never going to hit the wicket, and sometimes even found themselves playing and missing at something which would pass the off stump and gone on to be taken to the wicket-keeper's left on a line well outside the leg stump.

Colin Croft learned how to hold the occasional ball up and straighten it off the seam, and his overall Test record of 125 wickets in 27 games for the West Indies shows how, for every rule, there is invariably an exception. Furthermore, his strike rate of a wicket every 47 deliveries is one of the best in post-war cricket. Even the great Michael Holding's was one in 50, although he got twice as many wickets.

Generally, for most bowlers, the closer they can get to the stumps, the more successful they will be. The angle of line from delivery to the far wicket will be much straighter, and the batsman has to think about something else rather than just guarding against the ball coming back in to him. Also the very act of getting close to the stumps helps push a bowler into a more sideways position, and the improved

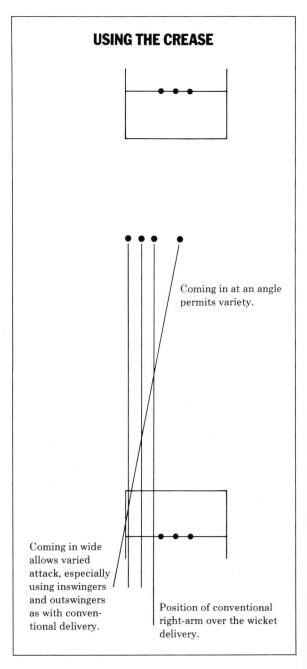

USING THE CREASE

Coming in at an angle permits variety.

Coming in wide allows varied attack, especially using inswingers and outswingers as with conventional delivery.

Position of conventional right-arm over the wicket delivery.

body action will generate the odd bit of extra pace and bounce.

I have explained how Tom Cartwright worked on his hand action until he could control that and his wrist, no matter what he did with his feet.

That is the ultimate target for young bowlers, but don't be put off if it seems impossible to master. Keep trying harder and harder, and if finally it won't happen, concentrate even more on what you can do automatically.

Every action is different, and the best bowling comes from bowlers who have enough of the basics under automatic control to give their whole mind to varying the hand action.

NO-BALLING Nothing is more off-putting to a bowler than to be called for a spate of no-balls. He is therefore worrying about where to drop his feet as he runs in to bowl. I don't bowl many no-balls—sometimes perhaps when I am getting tired and find myself stretching for the front line.

I find it difficult to understand how some bowlers who come off about a 15-yard run, keep on overstepping the mark.

Proper net practice should sort that out; although it is not just a matter of moving the mark back a foot or so. After all, even if you take it a yard back, the 36 inches gained can easily be swallowed up in a dozen or so running strides.

A strange sounding tip, but a useful one, for anyone who keeps getting called, is to go to the nets with a colleague. Then run *away from the bowling stump and let the ball go when you feel comfortable.* Do that several times, until your colleague can mark the place where you are usually letting it go. Now turn around and, remembering the foot you started off with, run in and bowl to the batting stumps, and you will find that you will have plenty of spare room at the bowling crease.

I have explained a few advantages of moving around the crease, and there is one more vital one. During a match, footholds can become a problem. Sometimes a bowler digs his own, or later in the match he will find himself in trouble with someone else's pit. If he is able to bowl from only one delivery point, he is in trouble because his whole rhythm goes; the bowler who can switch comfortably to another part of the crease, can cope much better.

WHY DOES THE BALL SWING? Swing and movement off the seam are the medium pacer's two main weapons, although do not forget the slight pace variations I have already discussed. If the ball is moving in the air, then concentrate on exploiting that for as long as possible. What makes a ball swing is still a bit of a mystery, although the so-called experts will talk knowledgeably about humidity, and dampness. Of course, they count, but there is still no complete explanation why, with every weather condition apparently perfect for swing bowling, the ball just does not move, and on other occasions, it can be swung in bright sunshine in a clear atmosphere.

Or why one ball will swing and another one will not. I have often seen a ball changed after about 30 overs or so because of some defect, and although previously there has been no movement, the replacement starts to go all over the place.

Sometimes a bowler swings it prodigiously one day, yet finds the next day, although conditions are the same, he cannot get it off the straight. That is when he must experiment a touch with the position of the seam by canting it a degree or so in a different direction. Never settle for anything in life, until you have tried everything in an attempt to achieve a particular aim.

FIELD PLACINGS FOR SWING BOWLING Back to swing bowling. If the ball is going nicely, make sure you have the right sort of field. For away swing, the slips and gully area need to be well-guarded, because assuming that you are drawing the batsman on to the front foot—*an absolute must when the ball is swinging*—that is where the false stroke will go.

An attacking field is bound to leave gaps, so make sure they are where the batsman is most vulnerable if he tries to find them. Leave the odd off side gap for the drive, and if your line is right, you should not need more than two, or at the most three, fielders looking after the leg side.

Make sure that your close catchers are close

enough to the bat for edges to carry. I would much rather see them too close than too deep. Nothing upsets a bowler more than when he has found the edge, only to see the ball drop short.

A good away swing line of attack is difficult to find and maintain, and again it is something each individual must work out for himself. A lot depends on how much the ball is swinging, but as a general rule, aim to start it on a line of middle and off. Late movement is the most deadly, and while a lot of bowlers find it easy to bowl 'bananas' which go straight from the hand, the knack of starting it all in the last third of the ball's flight is harder to master. Again that is down to hand and wrist action, with enough body action in support to overcome the trap of just 'putting the ball' on to the pitch.

If the better player starts to work out your line and is able to leave more and more deliveries alone, you must experiment until you make him play as often as possible.

Infuriatingly enough, a ball which will swing away from off stump, often obstinately refuses to do the same from middle, and stacks of runs are given away through mid wicket because of a bowler trying to straighten out his line.

A good tip here is, instead of moving your line over, *go slightly outwards along the bowling crease.* You are thus altering your line, but although the ball is still starting to swing from off stump the batsman will have to play at it because it has been bowled from a wider angle.

BOWLING INSWINGERS The inswinger is much easier to bowl for several reasons. Firstly, more bowlers have an action which is open chested, rather than the classic sideways one which makes the away swinger easier to learn. Secondly, the margin of directional error is greater, because on days when the ball is doing a lot the inswinger can be started from well outside off stump, and the batsman will still have to play more than he can safely leave.

As I have already explained, the shine faces the opposite way to the outswinger, with the polished side facing the off side for the right-handed bowler.

From over the wicket, even a straight ball pitching middle stump has little chance of going on to hit the stumps unless the ball straightens up from leg to off, so a swinging ball has no chance at all if it pitches on the same line.

A swing bowler really should spend a lot of time in the nets with no batsman to worry about, because then he will be able to see for himself just what deliveries actually go on to hit the stumps. The results will surprise everyone, and more is the pity that the umpires around the world are not compulsorily put through the same exercise regularly.

The inswing bowler will find that in order to hit, he will need to pitch outside off stump. Just how much can only be determined by trial and error. The two main factors to take into account are how much the ball is swinging, and the part of the bowling crease from which it is bowled.

By now, it should be obvious to all bowlers just how vitally important is that delivery point for the average bowler. An example of what I mean is that if an inswinger is bowled from the extreme edge of the crease, the ball will have to start on a line of at least 18 inches outside off stump; whereas from close to the stumps, even a line of off stump could trouble the batsman.

And remember that it is not the position of the back bowling foot which governs the delivery angle. After all, it is possible to drop the back foot right next to the stumps, and then splay the front foot down towards slip in a way that will change that delivery point by up to a couple of feet.

The other way round, it is possible to put the back foot down near the edge of the return crease, but still get the front foot well across and pointing to fine leg.

All swing bowlers should aim to get the batsman playing forward, but it is even more important for the inswinger, because anything played off the back foot can be watched right on to the bat and played away on the leg side with comfort.

Regarding close catchers, the right field is a bit more difficult to work out. This is because even though most deliveries are going from off to leg, at least one slip and a gully are essential for the ball that holds up and moves off the seam the other way.

It is one of the peculiarities of inswing bowling that sometimes a ball will move sharply away when it pitches on the seam. The bowler does not know how it happens, so a batsman has got no chance at all of anticipating such a deadly delivery. Imagine being careful to close the gate on the front foot against a big inswinger, which starts from outside off stump, only for it to pitch around middle and off and then take off like a fast leg break.

The away swinger sometimes does the opposite, but for some reason, if a ball is swinging away, the degree of reverse movement off the seam when it happens is never so pronounced. Perhaps it is because from over the wicket any movement the other way always seems greater. Often a batsman comes back to the dressing room having been bowled by a ball which he is convinced has pitched on leg stump and hit off. When he either sees a replay or asks the umpire or bowler later, he usually finds that it pitched around middle and off, or occasionally on middle, but rarely as far over as he thought.

With the seam for the inswinger pointing slightly leg side, the movement obtained in the air is more as a result of 'arm' bowling than a full body action. This is no reason to put less effort into it, because although swing bowling can trouble even the best players, they soon adjust to it, and the real problems only come from a bit of extra pace or lift.

FIELD PLACINGS FOR INSWINGERS This is why a forward short leg is essential, because apart from the chance of a catch from a lifter, there is always the possibility of the batsman not quite countering the movement back in to him and squeezing a bat–pad chance into that area.

At least one leg slip is essential, and sometimes two. The drawback in that is that the rules do not allow for a back-up deep fielder, and once a batsman picks up the line of anything missing leg stump, he has a free hit.

A deep fine leg therefore serves the dual purpose of making the lofted hit a risky one, and so increases the chances of getting a close catch by making the batsman play more defensively.

The good, accurate inswing bowler really needs at least five fielders on the leg side, and he must always have a mid wicket as protection for the forward short leg, as well as guarding the more likely run-scoring areas.

The position of mid on can vary a lot, depending on whether a batsman is looking to hit over the top, or how fluent a leg side player he is. For the real bottom-hand worker, mid on should be wider, and of course he is one of at least three men who are important when a bowler is trying to control which batsman is on strike.

If the ball is moving about, unless the wickets are clattering down and the bowler is right on top, he will usually prefer to bowl to one batsman rather than another. This is particularly so when a new batsman has come in, or when there is a right-hander and a left-hander in partnership.

In these circumstances, I don't mind giving the odd deliberate single away. A quiet way of doing that is to drop a few fielders who are normally positioned to save the single, back a few yards—such as mid on, mid off and cover point, for instance.

Don't make a big thing of it, otherwise the batsmen will catch on and refuse the bait. It is surprising how many bowlers will concentrate like mad towards the end of an over to keep somebody at that end, but do not give any thought at the start of an over to giving away a single in order to get at the more vulnerable player.

EXPERIMENT FULLY The follow through of an inswing bowler can vary sometimes, although I am not really in favour of the right arm finishing anywhere but well down by the left knee, having been swept right across the body as the ball is released.

But some inswingers find that when the ball is not moving, they can find a bit of swing by dragging the right arm down by the right knee. That is bound to open the whole action up, and reduce pace and hostility, but as I keep emphasizing: *no bowler should be afraid to try something different, if the normal things are not happening. Never accept that it is impossible to get any movement until you have experimented fully with the position of the seam, as well as your pace.*

Another mystery of swing bowling, is that the ball swings for a bowler one day at a certain pace, but he cannot do it when he bowls quicker. If that happens, then he has to decide whether the movement he can get at a slower pace has enough penetration to bother the batsman, or whether he will be better off bowling at his normal speed.

That covers the basics of swing bowling, and I hope I have shown what an art it is, and how there is always something to be learned. *So many people think that any art in bowling is confined only to the spinners, but that is totally wrong.*

The real satisfaction I have found in bowling comes from always seeking to widen my repertoire. From being a natural away swinger, thanks to Tom Cartwright, I learned the other one; then by watching him and experimenting myself, I was able to develop my effectiveness further.

I have never cluttered up my mind with theory, but instead, while I was learning, I would always just concentrate on a particular delivery until I felt confident enough to give it a go in the middle.

No bowler should ever be content with any performance. Even after I have got a few wickets, I think afterwards whether I should have got any more, or whether those I did get could have been dismissed quicker.

Approached properly, bowling is by far the most satisfying part of the game. Particularly when you plan for something and bring it off, or when you launch the latest weapon in your armoury at a batsman who thought he knew all about you and what you could do.

3

SEAM BOWLING

Now for a few words about seam bowling, which is yet another dimension of faster bowling. Some bowlers who cannot naturally swing the ball much, nevertheless have a hand action which produces a lot of movement off the seam. That comes because they make the seam hit the pitch in a vertical position more often than the average bowler.

An example of this is the Warwickshire fast bowler, Gladstone Small, who gets good players out because of his movement at a lively pace off the pitch, rather than through the air.

The former Derbyshire bowler, Mike Hendrick, was another, and of course movement off the seam poses many more problems to the batsman, because he cannot predict it. He knows that the bowler is trying to land the ball on the seam, so it will bite into the pitch, but he has no way of knowing when it will happen and, even more disconcerting, which way the movement will be when it does occur.

What a seam bowler has to work out is what length to bowl to get the maximum reward for his efforts. While this will vary from pitch to pitch, and also according sometimes to the batsman concerned, he is bound to have a natural length which is usually governed by pace.

Andy Roberts with a perfect seam position for the inswinger. Note the position of the thumb to the left of the seam.

There is one trap to avoid. *Do not settle for bowling slightly short of a length in order to avoid conceding a few boundaries.*

What happens then is that when the ball does move it usually beats the lot—bat and stumps—because it has a couple of feet extra to go before the batsman plays it. History is littered with instances of 'unlucky bowlers'.

I don't go along with that view, because anyone who plays the game long enough is never permanently lucky or unlucky. That always evens itself out over a long period, so if a bowler *appears to be always unlucky*, it must be because there is a flaw in his technique. In the same way, if a batsman gains the reputation of being lucky, it is usually because when he takes chances he has worked out a method of reducing the apparent risks.

So if a bowler keeps on beating the outside edge without getting a nick, the odds are that he is pitching it a shade too short. I know I have had plenty of stick in the past for apparently bowling too short, but that has usually been because I have been trying to unsettle batsmen with the odd bouncer, and not because I have wasted helpful seam bowling conditions.

It is easy to get carried away as soon as the first ball lifts and goes past the batsman's chin, but if there is seam movement available, it will always be best exploited by keeping the ball well up. Assuming that there is no swing, the batsman then has more chance to drive a few fours, but the quicker you dismiss any fear of that from your mind, the more wickets you are likely to take. I can think of far too many bowlers in county cricket who, once they have been hit for four, are guaranteed to pull their horns in for the rest of the over and just bowl for containment.

I work on the opposite theory. If I have been hit for four, the batsman is quite likely to have enough adrenalin created to have another go if I can tempt him; so while I may not serve him up the same delivery again, I don't mind offering him something else.

As movement off the pitch comes from the seam,

always make sure that it is kept clean. There are definite rules and penalties for illegally picking the seam, but the laws do allow for it to be kept clean. For instance, you cannot raise it in order to get more bite, but you can clean out any dirt or grass from the stitching in order to utilise it.

The ball is my main weapon, which is why I spend a lot of time between deliveries in keeping it clean and polished.

SOMETHING DIFFERENT As virtually everything I have said about seam and swing bowling has centred on the importance of the correct hand and wrist action keeping the seam upright, what comes next might sound like heresy. *Just occasionally, try a delivery in which you turn the fingers around 90 degrees and hold the ball right across the seam.*

Try that as something different when everything else has failed, or against a real tail-end rabbit, when a straight ball is all that is needed, and any seam movement is a waste.

That brings to an end the section on seam and swing bowling, and I hope I have been able to open up a few new horizons for budding bowlers. I note that I have dealt with holding the ball in all sorts of different ways. And also the shine, which I have suggested on occasions can be reversed as a variation.

The same varied advice has been given regarding position of the feet, and the more I consider all these points, the more convinced I am that bowling is such an *individual thing*, that any good natural bowler will succeed, even though he apparently has too many basic defects in his action.

Please remember that all my advice about the basics, is to help the average young bowler, but the last thing I want to do is to fall into the trap of so many coaches and spoil someone's natural ability by interfering with advice that is no good for him. On the other hand, just because a bowler is successful is no reason why he should not constantly set himself new targets. Here I go again. Self-belief and looking for new challenges give me more satisfaction and enjoyment than anything else in cricket.

4
SLOW BOWLING

There has not been a successful back of the hand bowler in English cricket during the majority of my career, and I suppose the dearth in this department is the most significant change in the modern game.

I have to admit that when I see someone like the great Pakistani leg spinner, Abdul Qadir, at work, I can understand the regrets of those former players and spectators who say that the game has lost a lot with their passing.

Limited overs cricket is blamed a lot, but as Qadir proved in the 1987 World Cup in Pakistan where he was his side's best and most economical bowler, any class bowler will pull his weight in the one-day game as well as in the traditional three- and five-day game.

What happened in England about 20 years ago was that instead of the odd overseas player being in the game—as was the case in the fifties and sixties—the Test and County Cricket Board decided to allow an immediate special registration of an overseas star for each county, and the clubs soon realized that what they wanted was a match-winner. Because pitches in this country have got slower and slower through the years, the value of the back of the hand spinner declined until he was just regarded as a luxury. So when the counties shopped abroad, they filled their baskets with fast bowlers and attacking batsmen, and an even bigger squeeze was applied to all spin bowling, not just the leg break merchant.

Think of how bare the cupboard is now, with the most effective spin bowlers like John Emburey and Eddie Hemmings almost without challenge in the England set-up. And although Pat Pocock retired a couple of years ago, he was still far enough in front of the younger slow bowlers to go on England's tour of India in 1985, where he helped win the series.

John Childs of Essex is another 'old-fashioned' spinner who belatedly got Test recognition against the West Indies in 1988, 13 years after making his county debut.

So what can be done to encourage a re-birth of spin in this country? Just as many youngsters want to bowl slow as in the past, but it is the view of the coaches that they have a much more minor role to play nowadays.

It has become a vicious circle, where the coaches are now moaning that no slow bowlers are coming through, but it is those same coaches who have blocked their path in the last decade.

For a start, I suggest that county coaches and committees re-appraise their attitude towards play-

SPIN BOWLING — THE BASIC GRIPS

The basic grip for off spin

The basic grip for leg spin

1 Concentrate on getting the maximum spin first.
2 Worry about line and length when spinning has been learned.
3 Remember to use variations.

ing slow bowlers in one-day cricket. Once a slow bowler masters the different arts of bowling in different formats of the game, the results might surprise a few people.

APPROACH I won't dwell too long on the basics of slow bowling, because most of my career has been spent in trying to smash them out of sight, so I would rather deal more with their approach than the actual technique.

The grip for the front of the hand slow bowler is well known, with the first two fingers of the bowling hand spread as wide as possible around the ball, with the forefinger laid across the seam to impart the spin.

Big hands are a great advantage, because the ball can be given a bigger 'rip'. The first bit of advice I would give the budding spinner, is to learn to spin the ball first. Never mind where it goes. There is no point in learning to bowl nice and straight on a length with a grip that hardly turns the ball at all, and then expecting to learn to give it a bigger tweak. You will, but because you will have to use a different grip, that hard-earned accuracy will count for nothing. So find out first how much you can turn the ball naturally, and then start to work on length and line.

Flight is an important part of slow bowling because the whole technique is based on deceit, with the spinner trying to persuade the batsman that either something will happen which then does not, or the other way around.

A lack of height for a slow bowler is not the great handicap that some people think. Admittedly, he will find it more difficult than a taller man to get bounce from a pitch, but he will probably have a compensatory extra 'loop' because he is letting the ball go from a lower angle.

Most of what I have said about the thinking part of seam and swing bowling, also applies to the spinners because they should always be planning and plotting what they are trying to do. And what form that thinking takes depends largely on whether the pitch is offering any spin or not. If it is,

the bowler must work out his best field placings, and here he must not go overboard on attack.

Mike Brearley was a dab hand at giving his spinners enough close fielders, but still leaving a couple of men in the deep as a protection, to act as a sort of deterrent against the slog.

Patience is probably just about the most important quality, although as in most other ways, Abdul Qadir blows holes in that theory. His temperament is like mine. He expects a wicket every ball, and just cannot take it too philosophically when a decision goes against him, or a batsman has a bit of luck.

Sometimes slow bowlers have to chip away for hours and hours, which is why it is essential they remain patient and persevering. As a general rule, the off spinner should always have a slip—even on a turning pitch, because the odd delivery will go straight through, and not always by design.

The 'arm ball' is just about the best variation in the off spinner's locker, especially when the ball is turning. Some bowlers work at it, and can bowl it almost to order—Fred Titmus was a master at it. But sometimes, even as shrewd a bowler as John Emburey tries to turn the ball, only to find it either goes straight on or even deviates a bit from leg to off.

Forward short leg is usually a must, with another man in the safer close-catching area behind square leg; and that will normally do, as far as the leg trap is concerned. A bat–pad man on the off side is useful for several reasons: if a batsman is concentrating on the orthodox forward defensive stroke with bat and pad locked together to negate the off spin, deflections off a false stroke produce the odd catch; and of course, if the batsman is worried by the possibility of that, he plays differently, and is likely to get out somewhere else.

Abdul Qadir, one of the most exciting spinners around, in action against England in Karachi, March 1984. Bob Taylor is trapped l.b.w.

Particularly with field settings for slow bowlers, a particular position can create pressure in more ways than one.

Usually at least two men in the deep are needed, and which part of the boundary they watch over really depends upon the particular batsman and the type of pitch. The firmer the pitch, the straighter mid wicket and long on need to be, because the big hit will not drag with the spin so much.

The sweep is the usual attacking tactic tried against the off spinner, so a man out deep somewhere behind square leg should be your best out-fielder, because he will always be in action.

No more than three fielders should be needed to guard the covers on a turning pitch, and the good bowler who has mastered a tight line, can make do with two.

Deep extra covers and deep 'sweepers' at square cover, should be non-starters because the only time either would be useful would be against bad bowling which gives too much width outside off stump.

A rule of field placings which should never be ignored is that *you should not set a field for bad bowling.* An off spinner only has a narrow slot to bowl into, and direction means so much.

Slow bowlers will always get hit, so the sooner they come to terms with that fact of life, the better. No bowler likes getting hit around, but the good slow bowler tries to turn it to his advantage, by accepting the challenge and trying to tempt the batsman still further, instead of taking the easy way out and settling for containment by spearing it in at around medium pace.

Obviously, if a batsman's eye is in enough to hit a couple of sixes, the bowler must not continue to serve up the same sort of delivery, but clever variations of flight and sometimes width, often do the trick. And I am not just talking about Test or county cricket. Earlier in this book I explained how Eddie Hemmings helped England into the final of the 1987 World Cup by refusing to be intimidated by either Viv Richards or Kapil Dev hitting him for boundaries. Instead, a little higher and slower—and

in both cases it was 'thank you very much, and well bowled Eddie'.

The off spinner cannot give it the same amount of width as, say, the slow left arm bowler, because of the direction of his spin back into the right-hander. If he pushes it wide of off stump, it will be virtually a free hit, with most of his fielders on the other side of the pitch. Anything pitching outside leg stump again gives the batsman too many choices. But with the left-arm spinner turning it the other way, he has a bit more scope if he is trying to get the better of a hitter.

Not many players can play 'inside out' over and through the covers, and the majority hit it either straight, or more probably, over wide mid on when they go for the big one. In a situation like that, don't be afraid to keep it tossed up, but make him fetch it from outside off stump. If instead you flatten the flight, it is that much easier for the batsman to cut you should you be short, and the pace is already on the ball to work it leg side if it is pitched up.

This is why my old friend Vic Marks is so difficult to slog about regularly, because he bowls slower and slower, and the batsman always has to put the pace on the ball. He is one of the few class spinners whose flight does not vary all that much in one or three day cricket. His field placings are usually much more defensive in limited overs matches, but his control of direction is so good that very few batsmen can take him on, other than in certain leg-side areas which he has covered. He knows that if he keeps the ball well up around middle and leg, the batsman can only play him off the front foot in a limited area on the leg side in front of the wicket, unless he is prepared to risk an across-the-line stroke.

That must be the aim of all spinners, no matter what the game's format. *They must always try to confine the batsman to playing into certain areas.*

In the limited-overs game, the spinner must make sure that his fielders are either saving the single or the boundary. Only on really big grounds—Bristol and The Oval, for instance—is there a case for any other policy.

5

BOWLING TO LEFT-HANDERS

I have left one bowling problem to the end of this section. It is the one of the differences and difficulties of bowling to left-handers, compared with right-handers for the majority of right-handed bowlers—and it applies to all bowlers alike, whether slow, medium or fast.

Most left-arm bowlers do not have the same problem of adjusting line, because for the quicker bowlers, most of their time is spent bowling at right-hand batsmen, and it is much easier for them to adjust when they get one of their own at the crease.

Let me deal with the right-handed seamer, bowling from over the wicket to a pair of batsmen—one of whom is right-handed, but the other is not. His direction line must vary up to a distance of roughly the width of the stumps, because while he is usually aiming to pitch on or outside the right-hander's off stump, if he pitches the same line to a left-hander, more deliveries than not will pitch outside leg stump—giving the left-hander all the protections offered by the l.b.w. law.

So, the only way to make him play is to pitch further across towards his off stump, and while most bowlers can soon adjust if there are two of a kind batting together, a left- and right-handed combination is unsettling. All a seamer can do is to concentrate even harder on keeping his head and eyes still, so that his leading, non-bowling arm can lead him down the right slot.

As a rule, I try to bring the ball back into the left-hander, more than trying to angle it across him—always providing of course there is some movement available. The reason for this, of course, is that if I pitch anything from outside a leftie's off stump to about middle, and I do enough to beat his bat, there is nowhere for the ball to go, other than hit the stumps—always assuming that it is not too high. I do not have the same area of width against the right-hander, because anything pitched outside his leg stump is a waste of time.

If the pitch is pretty flat then it is worth a go at exploiting what is supposed to be the traditional left-hander's weakness on and outside off stump. The ideal delivery will pitch around middle and off—straight enough to make him play, and just a touch of movement away off the seam might do the trick.

If nothing is happening at all, then I will switch to round the wicket. If I can get one to move back from outside off stump, I have distinct chances of an l.b.w. decision, or hitting the stumps if I can get through the gate.

Slow bowlers have to think firstly about that sort of switch from one side of the wicket to the other. As a general rule, unless the ball is turning, an off spinner will stay where he is and adjust his line a little further over towards the left-hander's off stump.

His field is likely to be a 6–3 split favouring the off side, but a slow left-arm bowler has one immediate advantage against a fellow left-hander. By switching from round to over the wicket, he can drop the ball into the normal rough which is always outside a left-hander's off stump. If he is accurate enough, he is unlikely to be driven because of the risk of a mis-hit; so he can crowd the batsman with a man in front of the bat, on either side of the wicket.

The left-hander then has the twin problem of avoiding giving a bat–pad catch, either with or into the spin, and as a result he might be forced into playing back when he should be forward.

As with the quicker bowlers, direction is all important because most left-handers are good sweepers, receiving as they do so much bowling directed around their legs.

SUMMARY I only hope that all I have said about bowling, will help someone to enjoy his performances with the ball as much as I have. Batting is satisfying of course when the runs come, but although often a big innings might establish the platform for a victory, it is *bowlers who win matches*.

One mistake with the bat can be fatal, but one of the good things about bowling is that you get more than one chance—*always providing that your head never drops*. To keep on going when the luck is running against you calls for guts and determination, so always make sure that you never shrug your shoulders and think, 'tomorrow is another day'. I prefer to say, *'today will never come again'*. Think about it.

Gatting, Emburey, and Athey all showing delight as Graham Dilley snaps up a crucial wicket on 1986/7 tour of Australia.

PART

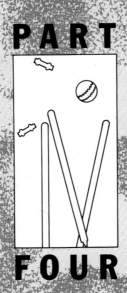

FOUR

FIELDING

1
APPROACH

I love fielding, and I regard it as the most important aspect of the game. Everyone is in the game all the time—not like batting or bowling when a mistake with the bat or a poor spell with the ball can put a player on the sidelines.

If you put your mind to it, there is at least as much fun and satisfaction to be got from fielding as in the other departments, and it is a part of cricket in which everybody can always improve his perform-ance. A great catch or a smart run-out—even a few good stops—can affect a match, and the difference between the fielding performances of two sides is often that between winning and losing.

My own approach to fielding is as simple and uncomplicated as it is to batting and bowling. *I love to impose myself by attacking the ball at every oppor-tunity, whether I am in the slips or fielding further away from the bat.*

Just think how many times an unexpected piece of fielding has thrown a spanner into the works by causing hesitation between the batsmen. That is why I never accept an apparently safe situation—instead I am always looking to make a yard in the slips by fielding closer than the average.

Away from the wicket, if I can change an appar-ently safe angle by swooping on the ball a yard early and throwing on the turn, just occasionally I can start that calling sequence of 'yes, no—oh sorry mate', which is music to a fielding side.

I am always being asked why, when I stand at slip, my hands are always resting on my thighs before the

ball is bowled. It is against the official coaching advice, which says that a player should be crouched right down low, with hands cupped in front of him at shin height.

Some commentators even criticize me for what I do, forgetting that I don't drop too many. Further-more, whereas in other parts of this book I have said that many unorthodox players succeed in spite of some individual habits, and not because of them, *in this case this is not so.*

I reckon that because of the way I stand—half upright, with hands resting on thighs—I am in a relaxed position from which I can immediately move in any direction. My speed of reaction, which is one of the secrets of close catching, is actually helped by my starting position, compared with what I regard as the too rigid posture advised by most coaches.

You see, as with wicket-keepers, the ball must go into the hands, and not the other way round with the hands going to the ball. Unless, of course, you have to go forward because of the danger of the ball not carrying.

I have fielded with some of the best catchers in the business for England, Somerset and Worcester-shire, and I soon learned that it is the relaxed field-ers who make fewest errors.

I couldn't have got off to a worse start when I first went in close for Somerset. I went there after we had dropped a lot, and I promptly missed the first one to come to me. What made it worse was that it was a lit-tle lollipop off the bowling of Alan Jones—it was against Essex and I think it was Brian Hardie. I was at first slip, where I don't particularly like to stand to the seamers, and it came to me so slowly, I could not believe it when I dropped it. Actually, quite a few slip catches go down because the ball takes a bit longer to arrive than the fielder thinks. This only underlines the point I have made about relaxing and letting the ball come into the hands. Try to imagine you're playing in the back garden at home!

Anyway, I caught a few after that, and have stood there more often than not since.

MY UNORTHODOX APPROACH The other thing I am often asked is why I stand at second slip so far in front of first, and if I am number three, why my position is so far advanced in front of second slip? After all, they argue that first slip takes up his position slightly in front of the wicket-keeper, so why should I vary 'the stagger' so much?

My answer to that is that I go where I think the ball will carry, and after all most 'keepers stand where they think the ball will go through to them slightly on the descent, because the last thing they want is to be forced into a series of 'takes' at an awkward height.

Also I know as a bowler that nothing is more frus-

> My approach means that I think of myself as a fielder as soon as I've bowled—which can present some unlikely opportunities.

trating than to see a genuine nick drop short. My attitude is that I would rather have my slips closer and perhaps drop one or two, than stand too deep. At least the first way, I have a chance.

Standing closer really came about for me in the late seventies and early eighties when pitches seemed to get slower and more placid. Now I always do it because, like a goalkeeper, I cut the angles

My expression says it all. Second Test, England v Australia, 1985 and Allan Border has just knicked one through the slips off Paul Allott. David Gower had just moved me from where the ball is now flying through the air!

down quite a bit. Sometimes it might look as though I am trying my hand at poaching if I go for a wide one, but more often than not if it is a real low chance, it would barely have carried to the other slips anyway.

It is another example of my individual approach to cricket. I have never done the orthodox and correct thing, just because that is the way things have always been done in the past. And similarly anything I do that looks different is not just for the sake of being different. It is because I have worked out that it actually helps me to bring off the unexpected, and that is where my greatest enjoyment and satisfaction always come from in cricket.

The more people who have a go at my technique and performances with bat, ball, or in the field, the more I love to prove them wrong. Not just to say I told you so, but invariably when I do something spectacular, the side benefits because I have been known to affect the course of the odd match.

Another example of my apparent unorthodox approach in the slips, is that whereas the average coach instructs young players to watch the ball from the bowler's arm at first slip, but at second or third slip he should watch the edge of the bat, *I always watch the ball.*

Obviously I don't when I occasionally field at gully, but that is a specialist position which I will deal with later.

The former England and Surrey batsman, Graham Roope, was another who always watched the ball, despite what the book says. Although every 'slipper' must work it out for himself, here is why I do it my way.

I find it much easier to have a better idea of the pace of the ball if I watch it through the air, rather

One Day International, England v West Indies, Leeds, June 1980; my first game as England Captain. Always try to get two hands to the ball if possible.

than shutting it out by squinting at the edge of the bat all the time. Also, that actually helps me to stay relaxed that little bit longer.

Anyway, watching the ball comes from the catching practice I do. I get a couple of the lads to throw underarm catches to me at varying heights and widths. This does not batter the hands as much as the more orthodox practice off the edge of the bat, and of course as well as making it essential that I focus on the ball all the way, it is also good reaction practice.

Even when I field away from the bat at mid off,

mid on, in the covers or the mid-wicket area, I still watch the ball. And also at leg slip. In fact, I suppose the only places I would not do it is in either of the bat–pad positions, close in front of the wicket on either side of the pitch.

The more I start to talk about my slip fielding, the more it seems I need to clarify the unusual aspects of it. Another one is the wisdom of fielding there while I am bowling. I know that the official view is that a bowler should get away from bending and concentrating while he is bowling at the other end; but to show once more what an individual choice

I am normally known for putting my hands on my knees whilst fielding but here, with two ex-England captains, we are finding time to relax with our hands on our heads.

most things in cricket are, I actually like it so much that I prefer to field there, no matter how long a spell I might be having.

Firstly, I have not got far to walk at the end of the over, and I channel my concentration into just the few seconds before each ball is bowled. Then I switch off, and perhaps have a laugh or a joke with the other slips and the wicket-keeper, or even the batsman. It helps me and my mates because it keeps them relaxed, and so they don't get tired or bored so easily if we are having a hard time of it.

I don't believe there is any great virtue in the

close fielders standing silent and stern-faced throughout a session in the name of concentration. They are there to snap up catches, and sometimes they don't arrive that regularly. The very act of maintaining unblinking concentration, even when the bowler is strolling back to the end of a long run-up, is bound to be counter-productive.

Sharp concentration and good reflex action when it matters will be sustained for much longer periods, if the fielders switch off once a ball has been bowled and they are out of the game, other than backing up any returns to the wicket-keeper.

THE SLIP CORDON I have referred to my advanced slip position in regard to people around me, so here are a few more thoughts on where, and how, the slip cordon should line up.

I believe that the aim must be to cover a certain area so that there is not room for anything to go through. Whether there are two slips, or three or four, the aim must be to cover everything, so I don't go along with the idea of dotting them wider and hoping for the best. That way, a greater area is covered, but not in a watertight way.

I have already said that, as bowler, one thing that infuriates me is when an edge drops short of the slips. Another is when I see a chance go through about knee height between a couple of fielders who do not even get a touch. This particularly applies to between first slip and the wicket-keeper, and the area between them is the most important of all to be correctly covered.

There is no hard and fast rule about how wide the first slip should stand. Not like between the other slips, who simply have to make sure that when they

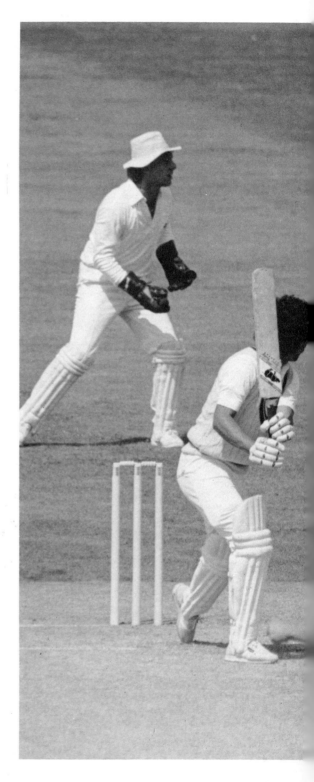

Note my advanced position compared with first slip, and also how much wider I stand for left handers, compared with right handers.

Had I been standing
further back this chance
would certainly have
been at a more difficult
catching height.

stretch their arms out sideways, they are close enough to touching to guarantee that at least one hand can get to any chance between them. But first slip and the 'keeper are different. They need to know each other and work out an understanding which can actually vary the width between different pairings by up to a yard.

As a general rule, anything to the left of first slip off a right-handed batsman should be the wicket-keeper's catch. He has got the gloves on, and should automatically go for everything in that area.

Some 'keepers are more agile than others, which is why the distance from first slip can vary so much. The great Aussie, Rod Marsh, always used to push his first slip as wide as he could afford, and was thus able to dive to his right with no fear of poaching.

Encroaching on each other is the danger among the other slips if they stand too close, which is why some time should be spent in discussion and practice to find out what suits each fielder the best.

Some slips with the safest pairs of hands never get off their feet, while others are more agile and love to have a go at anything. It is better, if possible, to keep two contrasting individuals like that apart, and then everyone knows what they are trying to do.

Where to stand for slow bowling also varies a lot. I take into account the pace of the pitch and the bowler, and also whether he is turning it or not. For example, I stand finer on a firm pitch to a slow left-arm spinner than I would if he was turning it. Not only because his natural movement is from leg to off, but also the very fact that spin is obtainable usually means a slower and less firm surface.

Try to avoid moving too early, because whereas most slip catches off the quicker bowlers are outside edges which come quickly, off a spin bowler the slip is often tempted to anticipate a stroke off a batsman—particularly when he is going for a cut. But when the false stroke does come, if you have moved, usually to your right, and he gets a thin edge, you have little or no chance of holding the catch.

So stand still for as long as possible, and more catches will stick.

Not many slip fielders appreciate the big difference between fielding to right- and left-hand batsmen. What they must realize is that, because of the different angle, the catches also arrive in a different way. For instance, off the seamers, the slips will all invariably be wider of the off stump, as will the wicket-keeper, with the ball being angled across the batsman from the right-handed, over the wicket bowler. Also more catches will arrive to their left, and the attacking stroke usually produces a faster edge when it goes wrong. This is because the right-hander is edging a ball which more often than not is angled back in to him, so changing the direction. But a left-handed slash is helping the ball on its path, which is why it is usually a sharper chance.

GULLY AND SHORT LEG I don't field too often at gully or short leg because they are both specialist positions, but just a few words about the different qualities needed.

Gully needs a pair of hands like a bucket, and if possible a fielder with a long reach, because he is really there for the hard-hit slash. My old friend Joel Garner had both qualities, and I don't think I have ever seen anyone better in that position.

A good gully fielder works his position out for himself, and other than making sure that he is appreciably squarer of the slip nearest to him, he must evaluate the pace of the pitch and the sort of batsman on strike. If the player likes to get on the front foot, he can go that much closer, because the false stroke will come to him off the edge of the bat, which is at least seven or eight feet in front of the stumps, compared with when a back foot slash is played. Then, bat and ball meet usually a couple of feet backwards of the front crease, and with the bottom hand in charge the ball is bound to come quicker anyway.

If the pitch is slow and the odd delivery is lifting, the gully should be even closer because he can then be ready for something off the glove or the splice.

Some of the most thrilling catches I have seen have come from cuts or slashes right off the meat of

the bat, and because someone like Garner has intel-
ligently gone deeper, he has had an extra split second to sight the ball and hold on to it.

A gully must always focus on the edge of the bat,
because he is so much squarer than the slips that it is
not advisable to watch the ball from the bowler's
hand, and then switch to an angle off the bat which
might be as much as 45 degrees off the straight.

As for forward short leg, not only has he got to be
a specialist, he has to be a bit crazy too. 'Boot Hill'
we call it and for obvious reasons. When a batsman
has a whack, there is no way of avoiding the bullet if
it has your name on it. Helmets, boxes and shin-
guards might cover a few eventualities, but there is
an awful lot of precious skin left uncovered, and I
never cease to admire people like Bill Athey, Tim
Robinson and other fielders who never grumble at
standing there.

West Indian slip
fielders—sometimes
called 'Death Row'. From
left to right: Garner,
Greenidge, Harper,
Richards and Lloyd.

This is one position where a low stance helps, and
not just because it offers a smaller target. Most
chances there are low and sharp, and the fielder
should be ready *and coming forward if possible.*

The great temptation is to rock back on the heels
when the ball is played, and the most successful
catchers in this hardest of all positions are those
who stand their ground and stay on the balls of the
feet while the ball is being played. That often makes
the difference between a chance carrying or not.

The eyes must be unblinkingly fixed on the bat

edge, and the nature of the chances are such that more one-handed catches are taken here than anywhere else. It is almost impossible to keep the hands relaxed, because the very nature of the position calls for them to come forward, but if it can be done, try to let the shin-high chances, and those above, come on just that little bit further.

Easy advice to give, and nearly impossible to carry out in what is usually a purely reflex position. If you do stand there, good luck, and keep your insurance policies up to date!

COVER AND MID-WICKET Before I get too many cricketers too nervous, let me get away from the wicket into the cover and mid-wicket areas, which play such a big part in how much control the fielding captain has. If he can keep an arc of three fielders on one side of the wicket, and two on the other, then he is usually in charge—particularly in the one-day game.

What I always advocate is that the best fielders should be placed in the best positions for the side. By that I mean that the best catchers should not necessarily be in the slips where most chances go. Take Allan Lamb, for instance. He can catch close to the wicket as well as anyone, but it is generally a waste of his speed over the ground and outfield ability to put him there. Particularly because he is likely to be in action more often somewhere else. For instance, if I am bowling and fancy setting a bouncer trap, I want 'Lambie' there because I know he will go for anything.

Not for him the 'stand back and wait' technique if he is unsure whether a ball will carry or not. In he goes, attacking the ball all the way, which makes me angry whenever he gets criticized for missing something difficult and low. I well know that a lot of field-

How best to catch at eye level; hands about to be cupped ready to 'give' with the ball.

ers would never have given it a go, and coming in at full pelt as he does all the time, if he does get to something, he has no chance of steadying himself.

CATCHING THE BALL There are different methods of catching the ball, and I have been asked frequently whether I prefer the orthodox English way or that of the Australians who reverse their hands and make the catch, baseball fashion, with the hands above eye level.

Depending upon the type of catch, I don't mind which way—it all depends on the angles. Whichever method is used, *it is essential that the hands are no lower than chin level, unless it is unavoidable.* Too much can go wrong when the ball drops beneath eye level, and the shorter distance it has to go before the hands come into play, the better.

The hands should relax and give with the ball, and always make sure that both hands are used whenever possible. On rare occasions an overhead catch is better taken with one hand, but only because extra height can be attained in this way. Providing that the pre-catch judgement has allowed enough 'steadying time', then use both hands, with one cupped round the other in a slight overlapping position.

Which hand overlaps the other is again a matter of personal choice.

THROWING THE BALL There is not much advice I can give about throwing. If a cricketer has not got a good natural arm which delivers the ball flat and low, it is rare that it can be coached into him. I am lucky, because I could throw the ball over 70 yards when I was 12, and ever since then I have always been able to get the ball in to the 'keeper in double quick time.

Although I have mentioned distance, that is not the real test of an outfielder—it is the trajectory of his throw. As soon as I spot a fielder who gives it a real high loop, then I will take him on for an extra run. So any fielder who does not have a great throw from 50 or 60 yards out, don't be frightened of bouncing it in—even more than once—providing the throw is hard and fast. Precious time will be saved, and just occasionally a run-out will result.

An obvious tip, but sometimes surprisingly ignored at top level, is *always to return the ball to the wicket-keeper, unless there is a chance of a run-out at the other end*. I have seen too many fingers damaged by a bowler in taking a return which should never have come to him. The 'keeper has the gloves on, so use him, and of course by tidying up the more inaccurate returns, he can also help to maintain the ball in its best condition, by keeping it off the ground whenever possible.

BACKING UP I started off this section on fielding by emphasizing what fun there is to be got from it, and one way to make the most of it is to make sure that you are fully involved all the time. Always be on the look-out to back up a throw at either end. Never assume that because the wicket-keeper or the bowler is behind the stumps, nothing can go wrong, because it can.

The throw might land awkwardly and take an unexpected bounce, or something might distract the taker. Not to mention those annoying occasions when a batsman unwittingly gets in the line of return, and a deflection results. Also there can be a deflection off the stumps after a direct hit.

So wherever I am fielding, providing that I am on the square, as soon as a ball is played into the deep, I always check and double-check that both ends are covered. And just because one fielder has gone in support, is no reason why another should not also get there. What can beat one man can sometimes defeat two, and I have seen more than one match lost because of overthrows which have been unnecessarily conceded.

Without doubt, standards of fielding have done nothing but improve since the start of regular one-day cricket. My era has always been a dynamic one, and backing up comes more naturally nowadays than it used to because there are so many more run-out attempts.

If I am at mid wicket and the ball goes to fine leg, the slips should cover the wicket-keeper, so it is commonsense for me to go to the bowler's end. This sort of thinking ahead is like the old centre-half theory in soccer. Proper defence revolves around anticipation and covering.

Similarly for fielders in the single-saving positions at mid wicket or in the covers. Don't slavishly stand in exactly the same position for different batsmen. A front foot player is already moving in the right direction for a single, so if I have been put to save a single, that is what I aim to do. I might move in a touch closer for him, and go a bit deeper and squarer for the back-foot batsman, because he will take a bit longer to get into his stride.

Some really fluent top-hand players are the most difficult to adjust to, because their placing is done so late. Again, I take into account the speed of the batsmen; although when two real dashers have got their act together, it is all but impossible to stop anything that is well placed.

IN THE OUTFIELD Third man and fine leg fielders are there to guard the boundary, so don't wander in too far before the ball is bowled. At third man, you then cannot cover as wide an area; and as well as that being true at fine leg, you also run the risk of a catch dropping over your head.

A catch off a fast bowler should never drop over fine leg's head, between him and the boundary line for four. Never.

Why I find fielding so rewarding is that there are so many aspects of it, other than the various positions, or catching and throwing the ball.

THE CAPTAIN'S ROLE Everyone should keep his eye on his captain all the time. He might want to make a slight alteration in the field which affects more than one player, and he will be wasting his time if he has to shout it from the rooftops. So watch him all the time, because a signalled instruction might mean the batsman misses it, and there is no obligation to keep him informed of traps being laid.

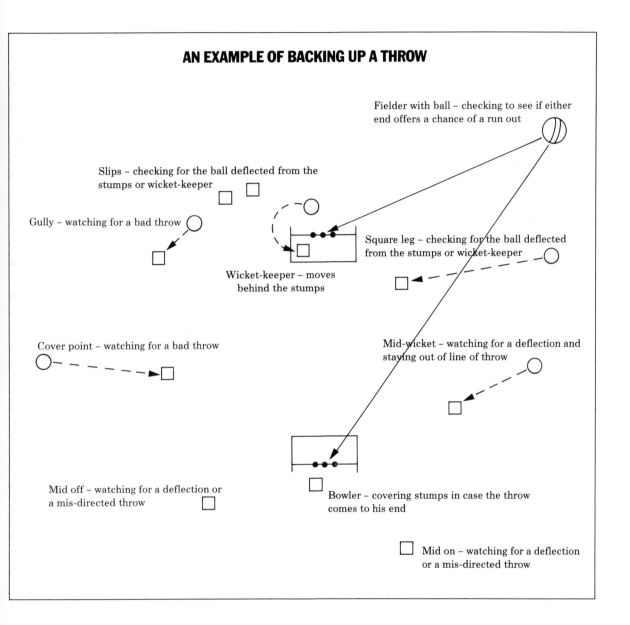

AN EXAMPLE OF BACKING UP A THROW

Fielder with ball – checking to see if either end offers a chance of a run out

Slips – checking for the ball deflected from the stumps or wicket-keeper

Gully – watching for a bad throw

Square leg – checking for the ball deflected from the stumps or wicket-keeper

Wicket-keeper – moves behind the stumps

Cover point – watching for a bad throw

Mid-wicket – watching for a deflection and staying out of line of throw

Mid off – watching for a deflection or a mis-directed throw

Bowler – covering stumps in case the throw comes to his end

Mid on – watching for a deflection or a mis-directed throw

We all know the trouble a signal got Mike Gatting into in Faisalabad in December 1987, but had David Capel at deep square leg reacted that little bit quicker to his captain's first instruction, there would have been no need for the harmless, left-handed, stop signal 'Gatt' indicated to the incoming Capel as Eddie Hemmings was about to let the ball go. Such a little mistake, but it led to scenes and the loss of a day's play—completely unprecedented in the history of Test cricket.

The main thread of this section of the book is really the same as in the other departments of the game: *I always look for attacking options—first, second and third. Only when there is no alternative am I happy to defend.*

2
WICKET-KEEPERS

As the most specialized position in the side, the wicket-keeper is the most important player. He touches the ball more than the rest of the side put together during a full day's play, and his performance can lift or drop heads.

I would not presume to pretend to know too much about the technical side of glove work, but I can explain a few basics which are common to all the top wicket-keepers.

The real art for them is in standing up to the wicket, because almost any proficient fielder can stand back and do an adequate job against the seamers' attack.

All good wicket-keepers must have a *still head* when they are in action. That keeps their eyes in line and on an even keel, and everything spreads from that.

Every aspect of the game I have dealt with so far carries that same message regarding the eyes. In batting, the head must keep the eyes still until the ball has been watched on to the bat. In bowling, the head and eyes fix the target. In fielding, the ball must be watched right into the hands. And it is hands which are so vital for any 'keeper. The best ones suffer less damage because they take the ball correctly, and you don't have to be an expert to notice that with the good performers the ball seems to melt into the gloves. That is because the hands always give that fraction as the ball arrives, and that in turn happens because they have been correctly

positioned on to the path of the ball, and there is no need for that tell-tale grabbing movement which is a sure sign that the 'keeper is trying to get himself out of trouble.

Mobility helps a lot in getting a 'keeper into the right position, and I only have to think of performers like Bob Taylor, Bruce French, Jack Russell and my former Somerset colleague, Trevor Gard, to realize how well they used the qualities I have already mentioned—of a still head, a good pair of hands and good reflex mobility. Not to mention the greatest mental quality of all—*self-belief*.

Above all other players, there is no hiding place for a wicket-keeper. Every error is mercilessly spotlighted, and he knows the instant disappointment from a bowler if he drops a catch. Which is why he cannot let his head drop. He must shrug off his first natural reaction of disappointment, because the very next ball might give him a chance to atone. If he is mentally disturbed at himself, the odds are that down will go another one, and then things will be even worse.

I played more with Trevor Gard than the others, and in my book he was one of the more under-rated players of his time. He did not miss much, and was as keen and dedicated in his pre-match preparation as anyone I have seen.

I used to help him, particularly in pre-season practice with mobility sessions which used to last only about 30 minutes, because they were so exhausting.

He would make himself a little goal, and I would try to beat him with a non-stop stream of low, hard throws underarm to either side. No sooner had he stopped one and given it me back, than it was on its way to him again in a different direction.

The throws would get swifter and more awkward as the session went on, and it did wonders for his confidence, when he discovered just what he was capable of taking cleanly.

Confidence is all-important to 'keepers. Just like every other player, they have days when their touch and timing are missing. All they can do then is to tell themselves that even concert pianists occasionally hit a wrong note. The one thing they must never do is to forget all the hard work and skill that have got them where they are, and they must stick at it for the sake of themselves and the side.

After all, a wicket-keeper is the focal point of the whole side—the one and only lynchpin. He can raise flagging spirits by bubbling about his work, and when a side is at its sharpest in the field, he can help it sustain the effort by his own work.

He also needs to be a motivator, and he can be a constant source of help to his captain by how he offers sympathy or coaxing to a bowler who is beginning to feel that it is not his day.

STANDING UP Sometimes I have been asked whether I mind a wicket-keeper standing up to me. I don't really understand the question, although I suppose the inference is that somehow that is a reflection on my pace and hostility.

Not at all. There are plenty of good tactical reasons why a 'keeper should stand up, apart from whether or not the ball is coming through quickly enough when he is back. For instance, a batsman might decide to upset my length, by standing out of his crease a foot, or even two. As soon as my 'keeper comes up either the batsman goes back to his crease, in which case I can pitch the ball up that bit further, or he has to take the chance of being stumped if he misses anything.

Even if a batsman is not standing out, he may have been getting forward to me, without any fears of what is going on behind him; whereas as soon as there is a wicket-keeper in his hip pocket, he cannot play so freely.

Even if the pitch is not doing much, the batsman will be thinking about not lifting his back foot, or daring to go on a little walk in trying to play me away

AN INSPIRATION TO ALL KEEPERS

'Remember how many times Bob Taylor would gallop down the pitch in a Test match at the end of an over to catch up the bowler who was walking down to third man or fine leg. A pat on the shoulder, a word, and the bowler's head would go up, and he'd be convinced that his last over was perhaps a bit better than he had thought and that there was a chance of a wicket in the next.

'A 'keeper is also the only man who can tell the captain exactly what a bowler is, or is not, doing. Perhaps he can see that something is missing in his action, or the bowler is bowling at the wrong pace for conditions.

'Armed with that sort of knowledge, a captain can then go up to the bowler and talk his language. A 'keeper starts each game at the nerve centre of the team, and he must always strive to do justice to the importance of his role.'

on the leg side. So he will play a little differently and more carefully—and therefore he is being forced to try something different from what he wants.

I don't think that a 'keeper should stand up if the ball is lifting or moving, because he has no chance of catching anything which is deflected more than an inch or so. That is only commonsense. As the top 'keepers are not show ponies, you can bet that if they do come to stand up to a seamer, there is a good reason for it.

The best wicket-keepers just keep going, irrespective of the ups and downs of a long day in the field. They can't wander off somewhere and keep a low profile, until it is home time. They are always in the shop window, and they must always come up smiling at the end of the day.

Watch the top men.

Rhythm also plays a big part in a wicket-keeper's performance. He must ask himself—am I moving correctly, and am I positioned so that the ball is coming to me exactly how I want it?

He is the one player in a side who cannot be given any worthwhile advice on the field, because of his specialized position. So he must be constantly analysing everything he does, and that is difficult to do because of the intense concentration he has to sustain for every minute of play. Almost every ball calls for something from him, and no matter how long he goes without anything getting past the bat, he must never assume that it is the sort of day when nothing will come his way. Instead, he must tell himself that the next ball will be a catch.

There is so much for him to think about, it is a miracle that at the end of a long day in the field he can even walk off unassisted. For instance, he is bound to get some inaccurate returns from his fielders, but it helps all round if he makes the best of gathering them without any fuss or long looks at the offender. He knows what he has done, and it does not help team spirit if the 'keeper puts his hands on his hips and shakes his head.

The other thing about tidying up the wilder returns, is that going to meet every return, if it is coming in too short or low, will ensure that the ball is kept off the ground as much as possible, and thus its shine and hardness will last that little bit longer.

Only small details, but it is attention to those which puts the top 'keepers above the ordinary ones. There have not been too many tall great 'keepers—the South African Johnny Waite was a rare exception—because of the obvious difficulty bigger men have in maintaining good reflex mobility. Especially for the glove work near the ground.

EQUIPMENT Appearances count for such a lot behind the stumps, and most wicket-keepers in first-class cricket take a pride in how they turn out. Clean clothes and pads are a must, and footwear is especially important.

The state of the ground should be examined before the start of play each day, so that the shoes which give the best grip can be chosen. Gloves nowadays are individually custom made for county stumpers, whereas in the old days the majority used standard issue.

The individual choice now allows for all sorts of preferences—perhaps leather which is softer or stiffer than the average, and different parts of the gloves can be webbed.

The modern pads also tend to be lighter and smaller than the old-fashioned ones, and that is only logical because they are so seldom in use if the 'keeper is doing his job properly. Also lighter pads allow greater mobility, and often a 'keeper has to sprint to short fine leg, either to save a run or, more important, to take a skier.

He should *never offer his pads at a difficult low return*, although I often see that done by lazy lads in school or even club cricket.

Bruce French, England
and Nottinghamshire,
having to use one hand to
reach a wild return throw.

ABILITY The best wicket-keepers are those who can maintain their ability and enthusiasm from day to day, not those who react to personal success or failure in a way which affects them so much that their performance suffers.

I have already said how important it is that the 'keeper's head should never drop after a mistake, but just as big a danger is if he gets carried away after a brilliant catch or stumping. Some 'keepers then forget how difficult it is to concentrate all the time on doing the basics correctly, and start indulging in all sorts of flashy things.

The best performers are those whose work is so unobtrusive they hardly attract any notice until at the end of the day, you suddenly realize that they have caught all their catches, let no byes, and every return disappeared into their gloves.

It is a dangerous job, physically. I just can't imagine me standing up to the stumps and watching the ball right into my gloves with some madman like me flailing around with an attempted sweep or cut—or even a reverse sweep. That is where the still head and eyes are so valuable.

Even more than an allrounder like me, I reckon that a wicket-keeper can turn a match more often than any other player. A brilliant leg-side catch suddenly sees the back of someone like Viv Richards, and apart from the dent that puts into the opposition's morale, it also does wonders for the bowler and the whole of the fielding side.

A lot of nonsense is talked about the batting abilities of different 'keepers, and whether this should be taken into account in selection. *I firmly believe in choosing the best wicket-keeper because over a long period he is bound to hang on to the odd half chance that a lesser performer won't.* Put another way, it isn't much use someone scoring a useful 20 or 30, and then missing a top batsman who goes on to score a hundred.

That is not to say that any wicket-keeper should not work at his batting, because with its heavy emphasis on one-day matches, the modern game

IMPROVING THEIR BATTING

'There are some good examples of how some really fine wicket-keepers have improved with the bat after starting their careers as rabbits.

'Bob Taylor and Bruce French were kept out of the England side for a long time because other players could bat better, but they practised hard, and eventually were worth a position at number eight for England as good supportive batsmen.

'The Gloucestershire lad, Jack Russell, is another, and within the last few years he has developed so much that after starting off at about number nine in the three-day matches he opened in the Sunday League and was good enough to get a hundred.'

calls for everyone to come in to bat at some time when runs are vital.

Not many 'keepers can sustain the different concentrations needed to bat well up the order, because it is so demanding to have a long day in the field and then perhaps be batting within half an hour if early wickets go down. Or the other way round, it is asking too much for a player to play a long innings, and then after perhaps being last out, be back on the field within ten minutes, when he has to re-establish a different sort of concentration.

The only recent player in English cricket who has managed this difficult double act is Warwickshire's Geoff Humpage, but I think he is helped by not having to stand up to the stumps all that often.

I count wicket-keepers as lucky men, although they might not agree with me. I say this because all I ever want is to be in the game every ball, and they are.

PART

FIVE

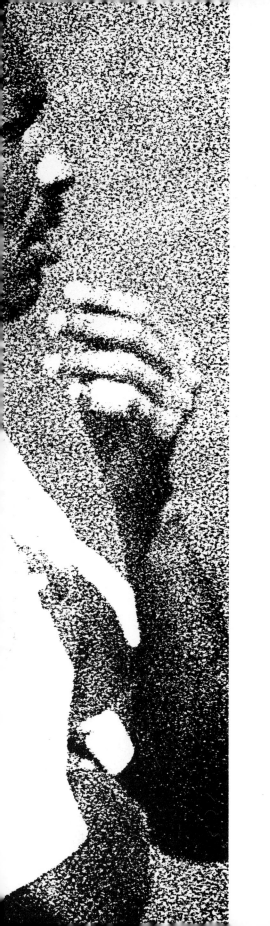

CAPTAINCY

1
HONESTY

Captaincy is based on a blend of commonsense, honesty and the ability to motivate, and I think I rate honesty as the most important quality.

I have seen too much skulduggery and backstabbing in a dressing room, and it has invariably come about because the captain has not previously insisted on complete honesty between him and his players. And it must be two-way honesty. I reckon if anyone has a gripe, then he should speak up to the captain or the vice-captain. I always do, and I have never regretted bringing something into the open which otherwise is left to smoulder, and then the whole side suffers.

That is how little cliques form in a dressing room, and then the side is just incapable of pulling together—which means they can rarely play to their best.

The captain runs the whole show, so it is down to him to establish the guidelines. He must show people that he is always straight with them. The first trap a lot of captains fall into is to try to spare the feelings of a player if they have to drop him. I have heard all sorts of fancy reasons given for leaving a player out, and often someone else is blamed: like a selection committee, for instance. 'I fought like blazes for you, but they wouldn't have it.'

The captain should always have the last say in who plays and who does not. What he should always realize is that the players know the final selection is his. They would respect him more if he told them the truth, and explained why he had made a particular selection.

Only a stupid man would deliberately saddle himself with a side that was not the best available and even if the player concerned did not think he should have been left out, he always knows that he is at the mercy of someone's judgement, whether that judgement turns out to be correct or not.

That is not the point. Despite what a few experts have to say, cricket captaincy has the one drawback *that decisions can never be taken with hindsight.* We can all get it right after the event, but the captain has to make up his mind a shade earlier than that.

The best captains are those who listen to all the advice, then go away into a corner and decide for themselves. I must admit that I have often led the way in the England dressing room when there has been any discussion about whether we should field first or not.

Every captain I have played under has listened, but whereas one man would still make his own mind up, I know that there is also the individual who can be swayed by what he hears.

Mike Brearley, who understood me better than anyone I have ever played under, was very much his own man, and would only take a particular decision after a team discussion *if he thought it was the right one to take.* If he didn't, then he would go a different way, whatever the majority thought, and that has to be right.

TREAT PLAYERS AS INDIVIDUALS The best captains treat different players differently, and there was nobody better at this than Mike Brearley. He realized the value of good communication, and he worked out how best to motivate each player.

That is particularly important with bowlers—they need to be chivvied and coaxed along when things are not going right, and persuaded that someone else will do better with the wind, or by bowling from the better end.

Keeping the attack sweet is half the captaincy battle, and to do that, the captain must know what makes each man tick. What spurs him on—how he reacts to disappointment, and so on.

When I first toured with Mike, he made a point of coming out with me occasionally to places he would never dream of visiting on his own. I know now that he just wanted to work me out, and although he was quiet and unassuming, he knew exactly where he was going as captain. Which is why he made such a success of it, despite the fact that he was far from being the best batsman ever to play for England.

It wasn't just me he sorted out on that tour of Pakistan either. He would make a point of getting each player in his room every now and again, just to see if they were happy. If there was something bothering them, he would talk it out.

Particularly on tour, with 16 players living, playing and travelling in each other's pockets for three or four months, it is essential that each one plays his part. Inevitably on every tour, two or three players do not figure in the Test squad, but they have a part to play in practising hard, and generally helping out in the dressing room.

It was only on that tour that I have ever been on the outside to begin with, and that was because Mike told me he considered Chris Old to be a better allrounder than me. I said he was wrong and later he was brave enough to admit his misjudgement.

I didn't like the comparison, but at least I respected Mike's judgement as an honest one, and it simply increased my self-belief that as I was the better player, I would prove it.

Back to those words 'honesty' and 'self-belief' again. How far I would ever have got in cricket without them being the basis of my whole philosophy, I will never know, but I have a strong suspicion that, without them, this book would not have even been thought of.

I have mentioned the advantage a captain has who learns to treat every player differently, and the first mistake I made after being appointed captain of England in 1980 was to fail to appreciate the necessity for that. I tried to treat them all the same, and although it might have worked on an easier playing tour than the West Indies, I certainly missed a big trick out there.

MY INFLUENCE

'In retrospect I had a lot to do with Bob Willis's decision to put Australia in first in the third Test in Adelaide in 1985.

'As Bob later outlined in his diary of the tour, he allowed himself to be swayed by the majority even though in his own mind he felt it was a wrong decision. Events proved me wrong and we lost the match, but although I still think my reasons were valid before the start of the game I also believe that if Bob really felt that strongly about batting first, he should have acted accordingly.'

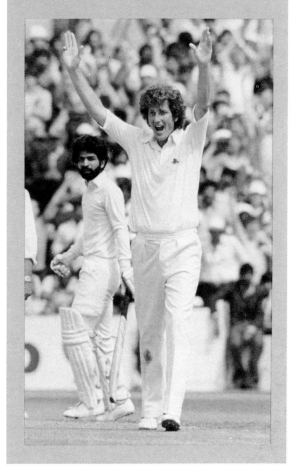

It was Peter Willey who took me on one side, when the tour was under way, and pointed out that I really did not know my players that well. I took the point, and I am sure that if I had been allowed to go on for another series and a tour at least, I would have done the job as well as anyone.

Mike Brearley, England and Middlesex, the best captain I have ever known.

2

DEALING WITH PRESSURE

When I lost the job after the Lord's Test against Australia in 1981, it was just about the biggest personal disappointment of my career. Looking back, I am proud of how I handled it. I did not dodge the press conference in the Writing Room in the famous Pavilion, and I told them the truth as I knew it.

I then had to face my family, friends and Somerset team mates in the next couple of days, but I was determined that I would not let it affect my approach to my cricket, and the record books show that I managed to bounce back pretty well.

The pressure on a captain gets more intense with each level of cricket. Even at school or junior club level, there are the same situations to resolve as Test captains are faced with. Admittedly most of the decisions at lower levels are cricketing ones, but the leader's judgement is always on the block.

Whether it is the batting order he has worked out, or perhaps because he did not vary it according to the state of the game; every time he is under scrutiny, particularly in the field. Multiply that a thousand times, and a better idea can be got of the sort of pressure under which an England captain now has to operate.

Television and radio experts dissect every move, and because they are paid to give their opinions sometimes they feel bound to have their say, even when there is little to talk about. Bowling changes are pulled apart and put together again, and when it comes to judging declarations, they have a field day.

They have one big advantage. In the same way as when they criticize the selectors, and their sides never have to take the field, none of the decisions they would have made, had they been in charge, ever get put to the test.

All the commentators and experts are not the same, thank goodness; but those who are thankfully different and more tolerant of the modern player, *are those who seldom if ever refer to the days when they played the game.*

I accept that they were all good, and sometimes great players, but what they find difficult to understand is how the game changes from era to era. I expect I shall have the same problem in 15 years' time, but I shall certainly try to show a better understanding of the players' problems than is often the case by some of the notable microphone experts nowadays.

ATTITUDE TOWARDS UMPIRES I have not referred too much to umpires yet, but I think that a side's success depends a lot on its captain's attitude towards them.

Again it comes down to an understanding of the bowlers, and so much of the cricketing demands of captaincy are made in the field. When the side is batting, the dressing room almost takes care of itself, and other than a quiet word here or there if the state of the game warrants it, a wise captain will leave his batsmen alone. Particularly at Test level, they should be capable of assessing each situation for themselves; but in the field, a captain should always be looking to try something different if the wickets are not coming.

This is why the captain must try to control his bowlers if they over-react to a particular decision, and the sooner he can defuse the situation with a bit of humour perhaps, the better it is for his side.

Even worse than having an upset bowler is to have an upset umpire, because he is then in no state to do his best, and human nature being what it is, he is quite likely to react subconsciously in a way he would not do under normal circumstances.

Any captain I play under knows he won't get any problems from me in that area, because the only frustration I usually show is with myself. Sometimes I will say to a captain before a session, 'Look, I've had a few good shouts turned down by him, and I don't know why. If it goes on there might be trouble, so how about if I change ends?'

He might agree or perhaps tell me that the other bowlers will be better off at the end I want, so I must get on with it. I don't mind that as long as I get full support, and of course, once the captain has given me the proper reasons for what he wants to do, I'll accept whatever he says as being the best for the side. My job is not to argue.

There are so many different aspects of captaincy, but the most successful ones are those who work out their objective, involve the side all the way and are always prepared to be flexible if things don't go exactly according to plan—which is most of the time in cricket, of course.

TEAM TALKS I have sat in on dozens and dozens of team talks, and I can only remember one match when everything went the way we planned it. That was when we beat Nottinghamshire in the Benson and Hedges Final at Lord's in 1982, and we did them by nine wickets around the tea interval.

I find it boring and depressing to hear too much about the opposition and what they might do. I prefer to talk instead about what we are trying to do to them. There are too many theories about the game, and a captain should always remind his players that they must play the game according to how they see it on the day.

The hardest thing for some captains to learn is how to avoid responsibility affecting their own performances—which are usually with the bat, as specialist bowler-captains are few and far between—for the obvious reason that they find it difficult to concentrate fully when they are bowling.

TABLE TALK

'Some of the team talks remind me of the true story about an old Scottish soccer international called Alex Jackson. He watched in astonishment as the manager laid out a pitch on a table and dotted players around in their kick-off positions, before he outlined his plan if Scotland kicked off first.

'He moved the ball to and from about five players and was just about to move it again when suddenly Jackson put his foot under the table and kicked the lot in the air.

' "What was that for?" shouted the manager.

' "Easy. The opposition just made a successful tackle."

'Exactly! Too many team talks go into too much detail, and the good captain will concentrate on a few general points. He will also appreciate that their chief value is to encourage comradeship, which is best done by concentrating on positive things.'

That was Bob Willis's greatest problem, because he loved to wind himself up into a cocoon of concentration which would last as long as he bowled. It meant though that in between his own overs he found it difficult to think about the other bowler and any problems he might have, so he used to ask one or two of us to keep our eyes open for possible field changes, etc.

Among batting captains, the most unlikely individual will find out that the job affects his game, and he just cannot shut out the overall problems of the side when he goes in to bat. Surprisingly, Graham Gooch found that out after just one season of leading Essex in 1987, and so he handed the reins back over to Keith Fletcher.

That problem never bothered me, either when I captained England or Somerset. The critics say that my Test form suffered, but I believe the reason I had two moderate series was because we were up against the West Indies in back-to-back series, and that side of the early eighties was one of the best ever in the history of Test cricket.

LUCK! I have already listed honesty, commonsense and the ability to communicate and motivate as four of the main qualities needed for a successful captain, and there is a fifth! *Luck.*

Like Napoleon said—or was it the Duke of Wellington?—'I don't want to know how good a general is tactically. *Is he lucky?*'

I don't go along with that all the way, because I know how many times in cricket someone seems to be lucky, but when you analyse it they have made their own luck. But there are captains who seem to have the knack of getting a bit of fortune when they most need it.

Where I think David Gower and I were a bit unlucky when we captained England was that we both had to take on the West Indies in back-to-back series. That is the way the Test calendar is cycled, but if we had managed to avoid that for a couple of years, who knows what would have happened?

TEST MATCHES A modern Test captain's job is completely different from that in any other sort of cricket. And that applies even to first-class, three-day cricket and the limited overs variety.

Let me explain. A Test match means just that. It is a test of one country's best eleven players against the best eleven of another. The match is played at a different pace and always under the microscopic scrutiny of the television cameras and the radio microphones. Even the toss is covered so fully that it is rarely a matter nowadays of 'heads' or 'tails', and 'we'll bat'. Now we see the losing captain slope off, while the toss-winner explains his decision to the interviewer. So much hot air is generated that when the game actually begins, it is quite a relief.

The opening batsmen know that their dressing room is looking for crease occupation for as long as possible on the first day. The first day of any Test goes a long way towards shaping the other four. The big difference between the five-day and the three-day game is that whereas in county cricket both sides are usually looking to contrive a result if enough wickets are not falling regularly enough to bring about a natural finish, the opposite happens in Test cricket. All too rarely does a side risk defeat to get into a winning position—unless it is the final match of a series and they are behind.

One instance of that was in the Lahore Test against Pakistan in 1984, when I was already back in England with a knee injury. Bob Willis had also returned home, and David Gower took over the captaincy for the last two games of the three-match series. We got beaten in Karachi, and then David led the way to a gutsy draw in Faisalabad with 152, and Vic Marks was second highest scorer with 83. David knew that Pakistan, under Zaheer Abbas, would not take the slightest risk in the final Test, but he dangled so much of a carrot with a declaration calling for 243 off around 60 overs, that he nearly pulled off a miracle win.

After being 173 for 0, Mike Gatting caught three catches—wherever he went on the leg side, the ball followed him—and Sarfraz came in at 199 for 6 with 10 overs left. That is the sort of one-day target the batting side would get eight times out of ten, but this was a Test match, and with Pakistan determined to hang on to their 1–0 lead in the series, they settled for a draw.

That sort of declaration is the exception in five-day cricket, which is why captaining a Test side is so different. In the field, unlike county cricket where you know that if the opposition are not bowled out in a day, they usually declare, you normally stay there for the best part of two days if you haven't bowled them out.

A captain's bowling strategy has to be different in a Test match. He must use his strike bowlers sparingly if early wickets have not come, and he will try to see that the scoring rate is contained. Once a side bats on into the second day, they will usually be looking to build a big total as quickly as possible, in order to give themselves as much time as they can to bowl you out twice. Therefore, containment means that the longer you keep them batting, the less time your own batsmen have to defend when they go in.

I don't ever like thinking negatively, but Test matches have to be looked at in the context of the whole series, whether it is a three- or five-game one. Once a Test match is lost, two others must be won to take the series, and with so many games drawn because of the pitches, that does not happen too often in modern cricket.

So a captain must make sure that his field placings are spot on. He must know when to defend or attack, and of course he must always strike the balance with his bowlers, between using the right ones for the conditions, and at the same time not overworking any of them, which might mean that their performance suffers later in the innings or the match.

He must use every fielding strength at his disposal. If he has a left-handed and right-handed batting combination to deal with, he must still make sure that his best run-savers are in the key positions— even if it means a bit of a trek for them. For instance, the right-hander might be a good cutter, so someone like Derek Randall would be at backward point. Then a single is taken and the temptation is to leave Derek at backward square leg for the left-hander. But the batsman might also be a fluent off-side player, in which case the fielder must move over.

One thing that all captains should try to do, but a lot seem to forget, is to try to imagine what they would least like to happen if the match situation was reversed.

Even in Test matches, I have been amazed at the number of times when I know England have been struggling, and yet the opposition has not recognized that the time was ripe to pile on the pressure. Batting just before an interval for instance, when I

know we don't want another over, and yet they have made very little extra effort to speed things up to get one bowled.

And sometimes when we are bowling, I look at the clock and think, 'Another hour yet, and nothing is happening. I only hope they don't go berserk, because conditions are so much in their favour.' Yet often they just plod on at the same pace.

So no matter what level of cricket captaincy is involved, *always try to imagine what you would be thinking if, instead of batting, you were bowling—and the other way around.*

Never accept the way a game is going, until you have tried everything to turn the tide back your way. Such a reversal of fortunes is much harder to achieve in Test cricket, but it can happen.

One such time when a batting captain should imagine he is in the field, is when a declaration is imminent. So many times, the batting captain goes on for that little bit too long—particularly towards the end of a long day. Yet it is elementary to work out that what the opposition opening batsmen want most of all, is to face as few overs as possible. In which case the few extra runs got by a delayed declaration are often counter-productive.

A Test captain must be a hard man because he has to get hold of his team for five days, and maintain drive and discipline to endure a form of cricket which never allows a moment's relaxation. That is not to say there is no room for a laugh and a joke— because I can't play my cricket any other way—but all my efforts are directed at winning a game, and then if it can't be won, saving it.

COUNTY CRICKET In county cricket, it often makes sense to risk losing the odd match by going for victory. Only rarely when two top-of-the-table sides are playing each other will both sides settle for a draw, if by trying to win, they might lose.

Wickets fall quicker in the three-day game, and almost regardless of the match situation, a new batsman at the crease should mean that the fielding captain can create pressure. The obvious way is to

AN EXAMPLE

'I have already said how I like Allan Lamb to be in the deep if I am trying to bounce someone out, despite the fact that he catches so well close in. But if I have an idea I can trap somebody close, then I will ask my captain to give me the best catcher in the key position. One such instance also involved "Lambie", at Old Trafford against Australia in 1985.

'I fancied I could get David Boon in the gully— another instance of sometimes bowling to a player's strength, because he is a magnificent square cutter. I could easily have thought to myself that I must not give him any chance to cut me, but instead I decided to gamble by letting him have a go.

'So in went Allan, and as the photograph shows, out went Boon. Why I look so pleased, is that apart from having nailed him for 61 when he looked set for a big innings, it is especially satisfying to pre-plan something and then bring it off.'

strengthen the close field, but psychology plays a big part. If a batsman is a particularly nervous starter and wants to get off the mark quickly, it pays to keep him on nought for as long as possible, by perhaps putting an extra man in to save the single in the covers or at mid wicket.

Also when a personal landmark is coming up, like a hundred, some batsmen get edgier than others. Everyone gets a little wound up in the nineties, but some much more than others, which is why some strange things happen—even to experienced batsmen.

Harper keeping everyone on their toes during the Bicentenary Test at Lord's, 1987.

NERVOUS NINETIES

'Warwickshire's Andy Lloyd got stuck on 99 for 15 deliveries in 1987 at Edgbaston against Northamptonshire, so what did he do? Just about the greatest all-round fielder in the world, Roger Harper, was not playing in the match, but had just come on as substitute. There he was, lurking in the covers. Lloyd pushed one straight to him and, like a rabbit in the headlights, set off for the bowler's end for that 100th run, which he fell short of—only by five yards!'

3 DEALING WITH PLAYERS

BOWLERS Obviously a captain is running the show, but the circumstances need to be really unusual if he overrules a bowler about a particular fielding position. He might ask a bowler why he particularly wants a man somewhere or, the other way round, explain why he thinks the bowler should have him somewhere else. But if he insists, just to show who is boss, all that happens is that he has a disgruntled bowler on his hands, and nobody wins then.

It happened to me in Perth in 1978 in the second Test, when I was bowling to Peter Toohey with the new ball one more over away. Even at that age—I was 22 then—I had learned to put myself in the other bloke's shoes, and having worked out that if I was batting, I would expect a defensive, accurate over before the big attack came with the new ball, I decided to let him have a few bouncers.

I had asked Mike Brearley for a man out deep. He refused, and of course the first one dropped just where I wanted him. I know it can be argued that if the fielder had been there, Toohey might not have played the shot, but in any case I would have had him thinking, and that is half the bowling battle.

Anyway, the next three were also bouncers, and they all went for four, so captain and bowler were not very happy—with each other, or life in general.

A smart skipper never falls out with his bowlers. In fact, a captain must always try to think like a bowler, and although it might be thought that is difficult for a specialist batsman, a big help is if in the field he imagines he was batting and what he would like most or least—and then acts accordingly.

That doesn't always work, as for instance if a captain fancies a particular sort of bowling and just cannot imagine that some other batsman might find it more difficult to play. Mike Gatting, for instance, with off spinners.

FIELDERS A captain must keep his fielders involved, and that is much easier if he has done the ground work in the dressing room. Like explaining why everyone should keep their eye on him in case he wants a slight field adjustment. He can save a lot of time and trouble by establishing which fielders will field where at the start of a session. Nothing looks sloppier than when a side gets out in the middle at the start of play, and the captain starts to tell each man where to go.

That actually helps the batsmen because they like to see where every man is placed; but if they are all in place when he arrives at the wicket, apart from the fact that it is more difficult to mentally photograph the nine fielders, he is also aware that he is up against a well-organized side.

The same principle applies at the fall of a wicket. I know it is easier and more relaxed for me as the incoming batsman to arrive at the crease with the fielders standing around having a chat, whereas if they are all in position waiting for me, I feel as though I am being hurried up a little.

These are only small points, but attention to them is just as important as with the more obvious ones.

A fielding captain should never be afraid to try an occasional bowler if he is stuck. It may not come off and a quick 20 runs or so go on the board but, as with all the other departments in cricket, *fear should never prevent something being attempted.*

4

ONE-DAY MATCHES

I have deliberately left one-day cricket until the end of this section, because it is the most demanding of all for a captain. The game is played at a hundred miles an hour. There is usually only one interval when tactics can be reviewed. The captain has to keep his eye on the remaining rations of his bowlers, as well as to ensure that his field placings comply with the mandatory requirements of the fielding circles.

And of course each game can fluctuate so wildly that it is a work of art sometimes to remember when you are on top and when you are struggling. In these games, the captain must get much more involved in the dressing room, and not just in alterations of his batting order, although this is important.

Everyone recognizes the importance of a good start in any one-day game, whether it is of 40 overs each side, or more. But a captain should never lose sight of the fact *that he must try to get his most dangerous batsmen at the wicket for as long as possible.*

It was that principle which got me opening the innings for Worcestershire in the Refuge Assurance League in 1987. Skipper Phil Neale agreed with me that in such a 40-over competition, there was usually nobody round the bat, and I could only really build a worthwhile innings by going in first.

We tried it in the NatWest at Chelmsford against Essex, but I got caught for 0, and on reflection, the circumstances must be right before there is such a major alteration in the batting order.

I did it for England in the World Series in Australia in 1986, because although there were also plenty of close fielders, the rules there made it illegal for the fielding side to have any more than two fielders outside the circle for the first 15 overs. That played right into my hands, and I was able to settle the first game in the final at Melbourne where I hit 71 in the first couple of hours. I also got a few in Sydney when we won the trophy for the first time.

A lot of thought should go into the batting order because in a tight finish a side does not want to see one of its slowest runners at the crease. Try to keep a left- and right-handed combination going wherever possible, because not only does it complicate things for the bowlers, it adds one more problem for the fielding captain.

The batting captain should always ensure that the scoreboard is showing the right score—and often it does not—and make sure that all his side know the rules if the scores finish level. Pakistan actually lost a one-day international they had won when Abdul Qadir was run out going for a second run they didn't need. There was an argument that the game was over when he had completed the first run, because then Pakistan had lost one fewer wicket than the fielding side. When he ran himself out, that brought runs and wickets level, and the match was won and lost on the faster run rate in the first 30 overs.

The big danger is for a batting side to lose its momentum when it is well on course for victory. The big temptation then for the dresssing room is to say, 'We only need play normal cricket now and we are bound to win. So don't do anything silly.'

The silliest thing of all is when a couple of quick wickets go—perhaps a run-out or a dodgy decision—and the later batsmen cannot pick up the tempo again. The fielding side suddenly find they have won a match that appeared long gone.

More than any other form of cricket, one-day cricket is tailor-made for the brave and the positive. There can be no draw, so whatever the odds, it is always worth a spin of the wheel. In the field, a cap-

John Emburey, England
and Middlesex, a wily
one-day skipper and a
good fielder in certain
positions.

tain has his hardest job of all. Unless his bowlers have taken a few wickets, he knows that the onslaught towards the end of the innings is inevitable, and he must not panic when the ball starts going in all directions. He should know which are his best bowlers to save, although this can vary as well if there is an injury, or someone got smashed early.

All he can do is to instil into his bowlers where they should try to bowl, so that he can guard certain areas. He should ideally try to field on the square so that he is close to the action, and his fielders can always watch his signals.

He must always have his quickest fielders and those with the best arms where they are most useful. For instance, John Emburey is not the quickest fielder England has, but he has got one of the best and flattest throws in world cricket, so he must be used at long on or long off whenever possible. And he has shown how a slow bowler can be the best one to rely on at the death, providing he is accurate enough, and cool enough!

The unfailing principle for a captain to follow in one-day cricket is that *he must pick his best bowlers*. The nature of the pitch can affect this occasionally, but not too often, bearing in mind how rarely any close fielders are posted. The best bowlers don't get rattled out of their basic line and length too easily, and are better able to stand up to the pressure that is inevitable in a one-day contest.

I feel sorry for young bowlers coming into this sort of cricket, because there is no hiding place, and they have to take their full responsibility, unlike the old-timers who could be nursed for a couple of years in the three-day game while they were learning to bowl.

'Embers' has worked out a method of firing in yorkers and even low full tosses around middle and leg, and that makes it difficult for a right-hander to play him 'inside out' to the off side. With six fielders used on the leg side, and very little opportunity to sweep, he is able to go closer than most to confining the batsman to the quarter of the field from square leg round to straight behind his bowling stumps.

A fielding captain should always be prepared to try to bowl a side out if he has made good inroads early on. Yet how many times have I seen a side reduced to about 100 for 6 after 45 overs of a 60-over contest, only for the fielding side to stay back and settle for a score of around 180?

Had they tried a normal field with a couple of slips and a gully, the chances were that they would have taken the last four wickets against a side who they know will be under instruction to avoid the biggest crime in one-day cricket—*using up the full ration of overs*.

Although one-day cricket contains many defensive tactics, I still think there is plenty of scope for a positive approach, particularly by the fielding side. That is the responsibility of the captain.

Another situation that is ignored for too long is when a side is apparently cruising in with the bat, yet the opposition set fields which are playing right into the batsmen's hands. By that I mean that if a side needs something like 80 off 16 overs with seven or eight wickets in hand, unless the field is brought in, there are enough ones and twos knocking about for the batsmen to keep the tempo going without any problems. But if a tight, single-saving field is set on either side of the wicket, the ball either has to be hit over or through the cordon, and an error or two just might be forced.

If it doesn't work, then the fielding side loses a bit earlier, so why not gamble that possibility against the real chance of forcing a wicket or two?

What usually happens in such situations is that the field is brought in much too late when about 20 are needed off five or six overs. *Do it earlier, and a surprise might be the result.*

I believe that the former Gloucestershire captain, Tony Brown, who later moved into administration with the same club before he moved to Lord's after a spell with Somerset, had an unfulfilled ambition to play a Sunday League season using normal fields. He reckoned what he lost in terms of extra runs conceded would have been mostly offset by the wickets his bowlers would have taken. *It is a brave theory. So brave that I am afraid no side will ever have the guts to give it a go.*

Most of what I have said about captaincy emphasizes the responsibility and pressure they always have to contend with. I hope I have not frightened anybody off, because although I won and lost the leadership of England and Somerset, I would love to have another go in top cricket before I pack up. Like a wicket-keeper, *a good captain is always in the game, and that is all I ever want.*

PART

SIX

GENERAL

KNOWLEDGE

1

WHY I PLAY THE GAME THE WAY I DO

SELF-BELIEF I want to round off my thoughts on the game which has given me so much enjoyment, with some random comments on the approach and philosophy of mine, which I hope will fill in any gaps in this book's explanation of why I play the game the way I do.

Let me start off with how I react to a bad patch. Firstly, I ask myself whether I am just getting out for low scores, which happens to all batsmen some time in their careers, or whether a technical problem has appeared.

I have only ever asked two people for advice, and the answers from Kenny Barrington and Viv Richards carried the same message.

The 1981 tour of the West Indies was my worst for England and rounded off a period of ten months in Test cricket when my highest score was 57. I had spent the time being continually battered by their fast bowlers, and what I was slow to realize was that although after a couple of hours I might only have scored 30, that was more or less par for me *because I was receiving so many fewer deliveries as a result of their slow over rate.*

So the temptation was to start looking for faults that weren't there, and this is where Kenny helped me before he so sadly died in Barbados. He used to hammer home to me: 'Don't change the way you play. You have got here in the England side because of your attacking method, and just because it does not work so regularly against these great West Indies bowlers, is no reason to start tinkering around. *You must maintain self-belief.*'

Which I did, although it was not easy with Michael Holding, Malcolm Marshall, Joel Garner, Andy Roberts and Colin Croft queueing up to let it go all day long.

The same with Viv. I said to him once: 'Come and have a look at me in the nets. Things are going pretty badly at the moment.' He refused, but instead sat me down in a corner and said that just by me asking him he knew what was wrong. He said, 'I know you, and you've suddenly developed negative vibes; otherwise you would never have spoken to me about a few low scores. You know what your strengths are. Go out and play to them.'

And both men were right. Both men had been through the mill at county and Test level and understood my concern. Both men also knew that when they had suffered in a similar fashion, they worked out for themselves that bad patches came to everyone, and providing they stood firm with the method and technique that took them to the top, the tide would turn.

NET PRACTICE I learn more by talking things through than all the nets in the world. That is me, although I accept that nets have a big part to play in the lives of some players. All sorts of good and great players never dreamed of missing a day in the nets—Tom Graveney, Geoff Boycott, and Dennis Amiss are three who spring to mind.

The man to whom I owe so much, Ken Barrington, seen here with Alan Smith during the 1981 West Indies tour.

I respect their attitude, but believe that they would still have been great players had they been less of a slave to that daily habit. I am equally certain that too many runs get left in the nets, and also there are far too many good net players who do not do it in the middle.

There is a saying in golf that 'everybody dances when the band leader strikes up'. That is a reference to the fact that no matter how brilliantly different golfers play from tee to green, as soon as they get on the putting surface, everyone is equal.

Well, the band leader strikes up every time you go in to bat. What music is played depends on how soon you get hold of the baton, but too many players accept the tune on offer.

When I reached international level, I did not think it was being boastful to reckon I knew what suited me best, and that is how I have operated since. Sometimes I know I will never convince people that just because I do not take net practice as seriously as other England players, does not mean that I don't care about my form or fitness.

I am actually scared to bat in the nets when other batsmen are practising, because I get put off by balls being hit into the side of my net.

I repeat that I accept that other batsmen feel differently, but just because it works for them is no reason for everyone to be forced into the same routine. That is where Mickey Stewart was so good on the 1986–87 tour of Australia. It was his first tour as Assistant Manager, and neither of us knew what to expect from the other. As it happened, we found we were similar in many ways, including the vital one of straight-talking honesty. He never tried to kid me, and I have always spoken my mind to everyone. So he would ask me if I wanted a knock in the nets, and if I didn't then he wouldn't make me. Occasionally, when I did want one, it would be on my own, with none of those hard, hurtful cricket balls whizzing around in other nets.

To sum up: nets should be used when they are wanted—not willy nilly; even though I admit that to some people they create a sense of discipline.

MATCH PREPARATION Preparation for cricket is an individual thing. Some players like to get to the ground well before the start of play. Again I am different, because 45 minutes to an hour gives me plenty of time to do what I want.

Mickey co-operated without seeming to make an exception of me. He would say something like: 'Transport for the first shift will be 8.30 a.m. "Both", you take charge of the second lot at 9 a.m.' *That is one small example of man-management.*

Rather than a full net session with bat and ball, I concentrate instead on stretching exercises. I am thick-set, and the former England physiotherapist, Bernard Thomas, always impressed on me the importance of stretching muscles and tendons, rather than going through a hectic pre-match routine. Perhaps that is why I have been so free from injury in my career, because I have always worked out what is best for me and other people have let me get on with it.

I suppose there have been plenty of those same people who would have jumped on me if my performances had suffered, but as I have repeated many times in this book, *you must believe in yourself at all times.* Not just when you think that it will be easy to prove yourself right, but when you know it is going to be difficult as well. *That is proper self-belief.*

Preparation does not stop once the players go back into the dressing room from the nets or their physical jerks. In fact, the last half an hour before the start of a big match is the most important and revealing of all. It is no good a player being physically ready and alert, if his mental state is shot to pieces. That half an hour is as totally individual as anything else in the match. One player might want to chat and joke around—I do for one. But I always notice what suits other players. Some like to have a go at a crossword, although when I have had a peek, the odd one has been upside down. Others disappear to the toilets, just to be on their own and gather their thoughts before they face the crowd.

I have actually seen a player make himself physi-

Mike Gatting and me at full stretch! I cannot over-stress the value of warming up.

cally sick, in order to release the increasing tension. That is the side of top cricket which the average spectator knows little about. He thinks that when the players appear on the field, they are all nice and happily relaxed. *If only he knew the jangling nerves which affect everyone in different ways.*

I have made a few references to golf, and I love the Fuzzy Zoeller story of how he knew an opponent was nervous, when he saw him circling a putt, and trying to roll up his shirt sleeves. The punch line was the golfer had on a short-sleeved shirt!

Team talks are revealing, particularly those before Test matches. At home there is always an eve-of-game dinner, while on tour we have a meeting which lasts about an hour. I usually listen to see how much is negative, and then I'll chip in with something like, 'How about talking more about our strengths—not what they might do to us?'

I always stress the importance of a positive approach, even if we do not happen to be the bookmaker's favourites, because more than one apparent foregone conclusion has been upset by a side who have come quickly out of the blocks.

On tour there are 16 players and no two are the same. I don't like going into too much detail, but if there is a young bowler, I always ask him if there is anything I can help him with. For instance, if Gordon Greenidge was playing, I would say how important it would be to keep it well up to him around off stump, because he is such a murderer off the back foot on both sides of the wicket. He is one of the great cutters and pullers, and it is not being defensive to limit his opportunities in that area—just commonsense.

Comradeship is so important on tour, and I reckon I did my bit on my last tour in Australia in 1986–87. I paid extra for a suite in each hotel, and the Manager, Peter Lush, soon appreciated the benefit it was on occasions to the whole party. There isn't much chance for privacy in hotels on a tour like that, and it was surprising how many players regularly came in to see me and talk about things over the odd beer. Phil DeFreitas was one who spent a lot of time with me, and I like to think I was able to help him have a good tour.

At the senior end of the party, David Gower came in once and actually said, when he was down a bit, that he was beginning to think he should give the game up. I reminded him that it was me he was talking to—the guy who played with him for ten years and had seen most of his 6000 plus runs for England.

Cricket is so much a matter of buoying each other up, and I am sure that having that suite was a big help on the tour. We had the odd party in there, and all the players knew that at least they could get away from the press and public if they wanted. In fact the idea caught on so well, that some of the Aussie players also popped in from time to time.

ATTITUDE Full-time cricket inevitably provides a mixture of good days and bad days. After all, whatever the paying spectator thinks, it is a job, and just like any other profession, days come along when, no matter what you try, things go wrong. And there are also the usual times when you wonder why you took the job in the first place. An office worker is lucky when this happens because not many people see him and how he reacts to that sort of situation, whereas cricketers are on show all the time.

What divides the also rans from the great players is that when the former ask themselves 'what am I doing here?', the result is an inevitable shrug of the shoulders and a resigned acceptance of the fact it 'is going to be another of those days'.

The positive player gets rid of such a negative thought even quicker than it came, and I have found that there is the same dividing line between the positive and negative approach *right throughout the game*—and other sports as well.

The player who can drop a catch, put it behind him and take the next one—that is who you want in a team. I have no time for the cricketer who takes the first offered opportunity to hide. He is an instinctive loser, and all through my career, I have tried to help those sort of players improve their game, simply by deciding automatically to be positive instead of negative.

How most players play cricket reflects their character, but the tragedy is that not enough people realize it. Life is full of disappointments, and the real winners are not those who have fewest, but those who come through their setbacks best.

Back to the dropped catch. There might be a valid reason for it. Perhaps the fielder slipped, or lost it in the crowd or the sun, or any of half a dozen reasons. The successful player thinks about it, decides on what went wrong, and then forgets it.

They are the people who realize *that they are bound to suffer bad days, and that they cannot always be sitting on top of the Christmas tree. Sport and life just don't work like that.* The cricketers with most character are those who ride out their disappointment.

I might have scored a few runs and taken a few wickets and catches in my career, but I have had plenty of downs. The biggest was when I lost the England captaincy, and I have already explained how I refused to hide away after I was sacked. The only grumble I had was that I believe the selectors did it because they thought the cap just did not fit. Instead, they gave me a match at a time, and hid behind my poor form and the team's results.

Anyway, I believe so much in myself that playing disappointments are easy for me to get over. Personal attacks are more difficult because they affect my family and friends. These sort of outside pressures are bigger now than ever, and former players and selectors don't really understand the problem, because they never suffered the same media attention in their day.

AGGRESSION Having made the point that the mental approach of most players reflects itself in their playing approach to cricket, let me deal with one of my main characteristics—*aggression.*

I am naturally aggressive in my approach to life. Always have been and probably always will be. But there are different ways of showing it to different players. With some I can do it with just a stare (or should I say 'glare')—others by just grinning at them. My aim is always to impose myself, and anything is fair game within the rules, providing that it is all forgotten at the close of play.

I don't mind giving or taking a few verbals either if that helps unsettle someone. That is part and parcel of cricket, and as even the old-timers agree, it always has been.

The point to remember is that it should be *controlled aggression,* otherwise it will be counterproductive. For instance, Dennis Lillee never wasted his time ranting and raving at me. He might follow through and have a quiet word which was straight to the point. Also, of course, Keith Fletcher will always remember what a successful job Dennis made of psyching him out.

My aggression boils over, in this case during the Fourth Test against Pakistan at Edgbaston, July 1987.

Lennie Pascoe was the opposite. He would always be threatening to knock your head off. All I'd say to him was something like, 'Put a proper sentence together and I'll understand you.'

I called him a separatist once, and made it worse when he asked me what I meant, and I told him to go and look it up in a dictionary.

Jeff Thomson was different yet again. He would sound off and make the odd gesture, but what the crowd never realized was it was all aimed at himself for what he thought was a poor piece of bowling. In fact, I only ever saw him have a go at one player.

Forced aggression is stupid. What happens naturally is at least honest, and all that happens when someone conjures it all up is that one of us will say 'Where did you find him?'

To sum up: proper aggression is acceptable, and comes from a non-stop unswerving belief in your own ability and determination to impose yourself. If I do something silly with bat or ball, everyone can see I am fuming. That is because I cannot accept that I have failed. I will not say to myself, 'OK—that's it for today.' It is not. I want to prove my point, so next time I try even harder. With the bat I have to wait; with the ball I don't.

APTITUDE *I am firmly convinced that aptitude grows from attitude, and any player's mental approach should be used as a springboard to a permanent attacking outlook.* Too many players seem to be intimidated as soon as the spotlight is on them in a game. They must realize that everyone is nervous at the start of an innings, or when he first comes on to bowl.

England v Australia , One Day Texaco International at Manchester, 1985 ; on the offensive once again.

I am, and so is everyone else I have ever played with or against. As I have tried to show earlier in the book, different players try to hide their nerves in different ways, and the most successful are those who use that extra adrenalin to boost, and not detract from, their performance.

Deep breathing helps, because the great temptation is to rush things, especially early in an innings or at the opening of a bowling spell. By that, I don't necessarily mean that they attack too soon, but because they are wound up, they rush parts of their basic technique, and that means they cannot produce their best until they have relaxed a little and settled down.

The tell-tale signs are when a batsman is gripping the bat too tightly, and making too big a first foot movement before the ball is actually bowled. And with the ball, a bowler will not give himself time to be collected in his delivery stride. Again I turn to golf for the best comparison. When the top pros spray the ball about, it is usually because they have lost their normal rhythm and tempo, and as a result make a backswing which is either too fast or too short—or even both.

The wind-up for a good bowling action is like the golf backswing. The best results come from creating a wide arc, and that is done by a full extension of the arms and turn of the body. If you don't get back far enough, then the unwind of the body starts before it should, and the result is a hurried snatch which is only hit and miss. So a few deep breaths can help relax the mind and body, and try to do them when you are walking in to bat, or when you are walking back to bowl.

The faults above are common ones, but they can be cured, even by characters who are naturally less aggressive than me, *providing they develop a realistic confidence in their own ability.*

Look at the number of cricketers who play at one tempo in the three-day game, but can stroke it all over the ground in a one-day match. The reason for that is simple, yet the players concerned hide behind convenient excuses. The truth is, that in the three-day game they are frightened stiff of failure if an attacking stroke goes wrong, whereas in a limited overs contest, the same criticism is rarely levelled at a player for seemingly throwing his wicket away.

Put another way, until perhaps the final few overs of an innings in a county championship match, when bonus points or the result of the match might be affected, there is little onus on a batsman to force the pace. He seldom has to bat against the runs per over equation which dominates the one-day game. So he subconsciously settles for jogging along at a different pace, and while that is understandable, he must realize that, while he is doing this, he is settling for second best.

Any allrounder should always reverse his role mentally, and once he does that, he will know which sort of approach unsettles his opponent most with the bat when he is bowling, and the other way round when he is at the crease. Once that is done, batting and bowling become that much easier because you can visualize what the other man least wants to receive.

Too many players think to themselves, 'This lad is bowling well—I must keep him out somehow.' A better thought is: 'How can I disturb his rhythm? How can I unsettle him so that his line and length are not so dangerous?'

It does not have to be a big hit. Stand a couple of feet down the wicket, and you might be able to drive him. Or have a word with your partner and look for a few quick singles. That way the field might be altered to stop those, and a few gaps will appear elsewhere around the ground.

Even if they don't, you will have made him try something different. As far as I am concerned, that is what I always try to do as a second option, if I cannot impose myself by my normal attacking methods.

Similarly with the ball, in the three- and five-day games, bowlers are afraid to give a few runs away to buy a wicket. That seems a wrong approach to me, particularly as when they get hit about in one-day matches, they will accept that because it is the pattern of that sort of cricket.

My whole purpose in writing this book is to show that the reason I can give full rein to my attacking and aggressive approach on the cricket field is that I believe that I learned those basics which did not come naturally to me. Therefore I am always confident in my ability to dominate a game, because my technique has stood up to enough examinations to prove that it is basically sound and solid.

Like most sports, cricket is littered with instances of players who come into the first-class game with a bang, and then fade away in their second and third seasons. This is always because the county grapevine soon works out the strengths and weaknesses of new players, and what a player gets away with once or twice won't be allowed too often by the only full-time professional cricket circuit in the world.

The English game is like a tug of war, with every player trying to eliminate his own weaknesses and exploit those of others. The winners are those who stay ahead of the game, because players with flashy techniques just do not last.

Always remember that balance is essential in batting, bowling and fielding. Even some of my unorthodox strokes owe much to balance. For instance, I have developed over the years a lofted drive which is almost entirely controlled by my top, left hand, *and yet at impact my weight is not on the front foot in textbook style, but instead I am actually leaning back on my right leg, even though the stroke is played off the front foot.*

The sole reason for this is because I have decided to send the ball airmail, instead of along the ground. To get the ball properly launched, sometimes I need to lean back as I hit it. But what I concentrate on is letting my left hand and arm lead the stroke, otherwise once the right hand comes into it, I am

Just doing what comes naturally: 1986, with New Zealand on the receiving end.

bound to play across the line. Then I either get bowled, or don't hit the ball very far.

Never forget that the most powerful strokes off the front foot are made with a bit of room between the foot and line of ball in order to allow the arms fully to extend, and so create the all-important extra leverage.

Also, never forget that the nature of the pitch governs everything in cricket. I can play against the same bowler on two pitches which might be a couple of yards different in pace. By that I mean that the ball comes on to the bat off the pitch at a different speed and bounce; so what works against him one day, might not the next.

Except against the real top-class bowler, I usually quickly sort out what I am going to do to him; namely, whether I am better off trying to drive him, or perhaps I will look to cut and pull. The better the bowler, the harder this is to do, because he is also well aware of what you are trying to do and will try to stop you. I enjoy that sort of challenge the best, and when it is a really keen tussle, we might both try the odd bit of gamesmanship.

The former Worcestershire and Warwickshire skipper, Norman Gifford, was one bowler who was always trying something to unsettle me. Sometimes he would turn and bowl from different distances in his run-up, and he was a master of all the slow bowling tricks of the trade. What I used to do occasionally, was to wait until he had taken his first step to bowl, and then hold up my hand to stop him, because I would say I wasn't ready.

He knew I was, and also knew that I knew *he knew* I was, but if I could get him grumbling, then I was pleased because I had stopped him bowling at the tempo he wanted. Only a little thing, but it is attention to the little details which sometimes pays off.

Tempo and rhythm are so important to all bowlers. The Australian fast bowler, Craig McDermott, had a good series in England in 1985, but within six months, he could not get to the wicket with any sort of flow, and everything else promptly went—body action, position of the bowling hand and with those,

the ability to move the ball around. But he worked hard at it, and once his basic rhythm returned, so did everything else, and he was Australia's best bowler in the 1987 World Cup matches.

For a fast bowler, the run-up is really like that of a long jumper. If he knows he is going to hit the board, he can then concentrate on something else, and real aggression can be released. The best fast bowlers in world cricket are those with the best rhythm, who always seem to have themselves under such control that the batsman knows that there is an extra gear waiting to be selected if necessary.

Michael Holding was the classical example of a great bowler who never seemed to strain for anything. As a result, he bowled remarkably few no-balls for a bowler of his genuine pace, and it all came from his ability to keep his head and eyes so still. That ensured that his run-up and action were so repetitive that he could concentrate all his mind on producing twice as many variations of pace and movement as the average bowler.

No matter whether a young cricketer bats or bowls, the more progress he makes the more advice he is going to receive. I have heard it said a few times that a particular player has been spoiled by some well-meaning, but badly directed advice someone has given him.

I don't go along with that, because I reckon that if an individual is capable of being side-tracked from his own natural method to such an extent that his performances suffer, then he would have failed somewhere else along the way at a later date.

The better players learn to sift everything that is told them. *Never model yourself on someone else.* You can learn from other people of course, but you have to believe in yourself so totally that if anything goes wrong, it is down to you and nobody else.

Adopt that attitude, and the excuses which echo around too many dressing rooms will disappear, and the benefits of that instinctive honesty will be many.

The more players who can end up playing the game *their way*, from start to finish, the better.

Cricket is a simple game that too often is spoiled by the over-complicated advice of people telling you how you should do things. As in golf, just remember that it is not 'How?', but 'How many?'

2 FINAL MESSAGE

I hope that I have been able to show even the most ordinary cricketer, how much more enjoyment he or she can get from the sport, if they pay more attention to attitude and approach.

I have been lucky in many ways. In the first place I was given plenty of natural ability, but at every level I have played the game—from school to the Lord's Staff, and then on to Somerset, England and Worcestershire—I have seen plenty of promising cricketers with enough ability to go a long way, but for some reason have not.

The difference between me and those lads is my determination to use my strengths and never compromise an attitude which has taken me to the top.

Too many cricketers see the game as a rigid discipline, but to me it is a chance *to see what I can do. After all, if I have been given strength and ability, then it's up to me to use them.*

In our completely different ways and approaches to the game, I suppose that Geoff Boycott and I have received more ill-founded advice, comment and criticism than any other pair of England post-war cricketers. But what the critics fail to see is that we both achieved what we have, because of our approach and mentality, not in spite of them.

The flaw in their views was that too many of them wanted me to play like Geoff, and him like me. History will decide who was right, but I like to think that all the explanations of technique and attacking philosophies I have given in this book are logical and flexible enough to avoid the trap so many coaches fall into, when they blindly treat all their pupils alike.

The best coach is like the best horse trainer, who after he has broken in a young colt, teaches him how to use his ability, and then gives him enough free rein to express himself.

Cricket is never a dull game—but too often the people who play it, are.

Dismiss the fear of failure from your mind, and you will be amazed how less frequently you fail. I have never been afraid of failure in my life. Ask those bookmakers who put those odds of 500–1 in lights at Headingley in 1981.

INDEX